12/29/04
10
5/04

THE IRONY OF FREE SPEECH

THE IRONY OF
FREE SPEECH

—

OWEN M. FISS

Harvard University Press
Cambridge, Massachusetts
London, England
1996

Library of Congress Cataloging-in-Publication Data
Fiss, Owen M.
The irony of free speech / Owen M. Fiss.
p.   cm.
Includes bibliographical references and index.
ISBN 0-674-46660-8
1. Freedom of speech—United States. 2. Hate speech—
United States. 3. Pornography—United States. 4. Campaign funds—
Law and legislation—United States. I. Title.
KF4772.F57   1996
342.73′0853—dc20
[347.302853]
96-8289

To Brenda, Emily, and Gina Fiss
for their love, each in her own way

CONTENTS

—

THE IRONY OF FREE SPEECH

INTRODUCTION

—

Freedom of speech is among our most cherished rights, yet it has always been a contested domain. For most of this century it has been the subject of countless judicial battles and has sharply divided the Supreme Court. Indeed, the *Pentagon Papers* case of the early 1970s was one of the most fractious episodes in all Supreme Court history, involving a dispute between the Attorney General of the United States and two highly respected newspapers, the *New York Times* and *Washington Post,* and it left the Justices at odds with one another. Freedom of speech has also been fiercely debated within political circles, on the campuses of the nation, and even around the dinner table—in contexts ranging from the 1921 trial of Sacco and Vanzetti to the anti-Communist crusade of the 1950s.

To some observers, the current controversies over freedom of speech may not seem especially noteworthy; they may even be a bit tiresome. The issues may have changed—instead of subversion and the alleged Communist menace, we now are preoccupied with such topics as hate speech and campaign finance—yet the divisions and passion they engender are all too familiar. I believe, however, that such a perspective on today's free speech controversies—seeing them as nothing more than a repetition of the past—is mistaken. Something much deeper and much more significant is occurring. We are being invited, indeed required, to re-examine the nature of the modern state and to see whether it has any role in preserving our most basic freedoms.

The debates of the past were premised on the view that the state was the natural enemy of freedom. It was the state that was trying to silence the individual speaker, and it was the state that had to be curbed. There is much wisdom to this view, but it represents only a half truth. Surely, the state may be an oppressor, but it may also be a source of freedom. By considering a wide variety of the free speech controversies now in the headlines—hate speech, pornography, campaign finance, public funding of the arts, and the effort to gain access to the mass media—I will try to explain why the traditional presumption against the state is misleading and how the state might become the friend, rather than the enemy, of freedom.

This view—disquieting to some—rests on a number of premises. One is the impact that private aggregations of power have upon our freedom; sometimes the state is needed simply to counteract these forces. Even more fundamentally, this view is predicated on a theory of the First Amendment and its guarantee of free speech that emphasizes social, rather than individualistic, values. The freedom the state may be called upon to foster is a public freedom. Although some view the First Amendment as a protection of the individual interest in self-expression, a far more plausible theory, first formulated by Alexander Meiklejohn[1] and now embraced all along the political spectrum, from Robert Bork[2] to William Brennan,[3] views the First Amendment as a protection of popular sovereignty.

The law's intention is to broaden the terms of public discussion as a way of enabling common citizens to become aware of the issues before them and of the arguments on all sides and thus to pursue their ends fully and freely. A distinction is thus drawn between a libertarian and a democratic theory of speech, and it is the latter that impels my inquiry into the ways the state may enhance our freedom.

The libertarian view—that the First Amendment is a protection of self-expression—makes its appeal to the individualistic ethos that so dominates our popular and political culture. Free speech is seen as analogous to religious liberty, which is also protected by the First Amendment. Yet this theory is unable to explain why the interests of speakers should take priority over the interests of those individuals who are discussed in the speech, or who must listen to the speech, when those two sets of interests conflict. Nor is it able to explain why the right of free speech should extend to the many institutions and organizations—CBS, NAACP, ACLU, First National Bank of Boston, Pacific Gas & Electric, Turner Broadcasting System, VFW—that are routinely protected under the First Amendment, despite the fact that they do not directly represent the individual interest in self-expression. Speech is valued so importantly in the Constitution, I maintain, not because it is a form of self-expression or self-actualization but rather because it is essential for collective self-determination. Democracy allows the people to choose the form of life they wish to live and presupposes that this choice is made against a background of public debate that is, to use the now famous formula of Justice Brennan, "uninhibited, robust, and wide-open."[4]

In some instances, instrumentalities of the state will try to stifle free and open debate, and the First Amendment is the tried-and-true mechanism that stops or prevents such abuses of state power. In other instances, however, the state may have to act to further the robustness of public debate in circumstances where powers outside the state are stifling speech. It may have to allocate public resources—hand out megaphones—to those whose voices would not otherwise be heard in the public square. It may even have to silence the voices of some in order to hear the voices of the others. Sometimes there is simply no other way. The burden of this book is to explore when such exercises of the state's power to allocate and regulate are necessary, and how they might be reconciled with, indeed supported by, the First Amendment.

THE SILENCING EFFECT OF SPEECH

1

The First Amendment—almost magisterial in its simplicity—is often taken as the apotheosis of the classical liberal demand that the powers of the state be limited. It provides that "Congress shall make no law . . . abridging the freedom of speech, or of the press." The Supreme Court has read this provision not as an absolute bar to state regulation of speech but more in the nature of a mandate to draw a narrow boundary around the state's authority.

The precise location of this boundary has varied from age to age and from Court to Court, and even from Justice to Justice, but its position has always reflected a balance of two conflicting interests—the value of free expression versus the interests advanced by the state to support regulation (the so-called countervalues). Sometimes the accommodation of conflicting interests has been achieved through the promulgation of a number of categories of speech that may be subject to regulation. For example, the state has been allowed to regulate "fighting words" but not the "general advocacy of ideas." In other cases, the Court engaged in a more open and explicit balancing process in weighing the state's interest against that of free speech. The rule that allows the state to suppress speech that poses a "clear and present danger" to a vital state interest might be the best example of this approach. In either instance, the Court has tried, sometimes more successfully than others, to attend to both value and countervalue and to seek an accommodation of the two.

In trying to guide the Court in this process, Harry Kalven, Jr.—in my eyes the leading First Amendment scholar of the modern period—pleaded with the Court to remember that freedom of speech is not "a luxury civil liberty."[1] In a more jocular mood, he expressed the same sentiment in saying, "Honor the countervalues."[2] Kalven was an ardent defender of liberal values, always in favor of limiting the state, yet he felt that in its resolve to protect speech, the Court should not in any way trivialize the interests of the state. At the end of the day, speech might well win, indeed, speech *should* win. But not, Kalven insisted, before the Court gave a sympathetic hearing to what the state was trying to accomplish. The Court must begin by attending to the state's interests and treating them as fully worthy of respect.

The 1960s was an extraordinary period of American law, a glorious reminder of all that it might accomplish. The decade was best known for progress made in racial equality and the reform of the criminal process, but it was also marked by a number of notable free speech victories. When, in his book *A Worthy Tradition,* Kalven celebrated the evolution of First Amendment doctrine over the course of the twentieth century as an example of the law working itself pure, he was referring above all to the free speech decisions of the Warren Court in the 1960s. Although I am sympathetic to this reading of the sixties, I cannot help but wonder whether the free speech decisions of that era represented a fair test of Kalven's faith that speech would win even if the Court honored the counter-values.

Take the Court's repeated willingness to protect the protest activities of the Southern civil rights movement.[3] In those cases, the Southern states defended their actions in curbing free speech on the ground that they were attempting to preserve order. The Supreme Court listened to that defense with some measure of seriousness, but the plea on behalf of maintaining order was impeached by the racial policies the states were pursuing in the name of that value. Order did not just mean order, but order that preserves segregation. Then, in the years following the Watts riots in Los Angeles in 1965 and the emergence of the black power movement, the claims of order became somewhat distinct from the program of preserving segregation. In that context the countervalue, order, could be engaged more sympathetically, but at the risk that free speech would not prevail. For example, in *Walker v. City of Birmingham*, a majority of the Justices upheld a criminal contempt citation against Dr. Martin Luther King Jr. and his followers for parading in defiance of a restraining order, even though the state court had not given him an adequate opportunity to attack that order on free speech grounds.[4] The case arose in 1963, but the Justices spoke in the different circumstances of 1967 and were guided by the events that they saw before them then.

In truth, most of the Warren Court's First Amendment docket involved cases in which the countervalue advanced by the state was neither particularly alluring nor compelling, and for that reason the Court's decisions in favor of free speech generated widespread support. Examples are such landmarks as *New York Times v. Sullivan* (1964), *Brandenburg v. Ohio* (1969), and even, if it can be included within the reaches of the Warren Court, the *Pentagon Papers* case (1971). Like the early civil rights protest cases, these decisions are indeed important free speech victories, in that an opposite result would have been a profound setback for the cause of freedom. But at the same time we should recognize that these cases were not a true test of Kalven's faith that free speech would prevail.

In *New York Times v. Sullivan,* the Court curbed the state's capacity to protect reputation, but in fact the reputational interest in jeopardy was that of public officials, who, in the Court's view, necessarily assumed certain risks to their reputation when they entered the political fray.[5] In *Brandenburg v. Ohio,* the Court protected the advocacy of illegal conduct and tightened up the "clear and present danger" test, but it did so in a context devoid of any true danger;[6] the case involved a sparsely attended Klan rally in an isolated farm in Ohio. In the *Pentagon Papers* case the Court refused to give the Attorney General the injunction he sought against the publication of a Department of Defense document that was said to threaten national security.[7] Kalven marveled at the fact that this decision was handed down even when the nation was at war.[8] But there was less to the countervailing claim of national security advanced by the Attorney General than first met the eye. Although the document in question was based on classified documents and was itself classified as "Top Secret," in truth it consisted of nothing more than a historical study of our involvement in Vietnam up until 1968. Moreover, the war was unpopular in many quarters; most of the study was in the public domain by the time the Court spoke; and though the Court did in fact deny the government an injunction against further publication, a majority of the Justices made clear that the government could protect a legitimate interest in secrecy by use of the criminal law.

The situation is, however, entirely different with three of the free speech issues that dominate public discussion today—

hate speech, pornography, and campaign finance. They strain, indeed shatter, the liberal consensus because the countervalues offered by the state have an unusually compelling quality. These contemporary issues are a truer test of Kalven's faith in the ability of free speech to prevail over the countervalues.

IN A MOST decisive manner, the American constitutional order and its governing political philosophy were reshaped by *Brown v. Board of Education*[9] and the transformations that followed. Whereas the liberalism of the nineteenth century was defined by the claims of individual liberty and resulted in an unequivocal demand for limited government, the liberalism of today embraces the value of equality as well as liberty. Furthermore, contemporary liberalism acknowledges the role the state might play in securing equality and sometimes even liberty. Admittedly, *Roe v. Wade*[10] and its condemnation of the criminalization of abortion have given new vitality to the claims of individual liberty, but never, I would insist, to the exclusion of equality. Indeed, as most commentators and a number of the Justices now recognize, *Roe v. Wade* is not fully explicable as a matter of constitutional theory unless some account is taken of equality and the consequences that criminalizing abortion would have upon the social status of women.[11]

This transformation of the constitutional order and of liberalism itself was not the work of the Supreme Court alone. In the 1960s all branches of government coordinated their efforts and produced such singular measures as the Civil Rights Act of 1964, the Voting Rights Act of 1965, and the Civil Rights Act of 1968.[12] In the ensuing decades, as the Court and the presidency moved to the right, the leadership role fell to Congress.[13] The momentum toward equal treatment continued even during the Reagan and Bush years and resulted in the

Voting Rights Act of 1982, the Americans with Disabilities Act of 1990, and the Civil Rights Act of 1991.[14]

As a result of these developments, more and more spheres of human activity—voting, education, housing, employment, transportation—have come to be covered by antidiscrimination law, so that today there is virtually no public activity of any significance that is beyond its reach. Moreover, the protection of the law has been extended to a wide array of disadvantaged groups—racial, religious and ethnic minorities, women, the disabled. Soon it is likely to be extended to groups defined by their sexual orientation. Over the last forty or fifty years, civil rights laws have become essential to the American legal order.

The welfare policies of the modern state fall short of the lofty ambitions proclaimed by those who launched the War on Poverty in the 1960s. Today we are more tolerant of economic inequalities. But norms protecting the poor against discrimination still have their force in certain special domains, such as the criminal and electoral processes.[15] Moreover, despite repeated assaults over the last twenty-five years, contemporary liberalism remains committed to satisfying the minimum needs of the economically downtrodden, providing them, though sometimes inadequately, with access to food, housing, and medical care. Like the civil rights measures, these welfare policies are actively embraced by contemporary liberalism.

Against this background, it is no surprise that in confronting the regulation of hate speech, pornography, and campaign finance today, many liberals find it difficult to choose freedom of speech over the countervalues being threatened. The liberals' commitment to speech remains strong, as evidenced by their staunch support for the flag-burning decisions,[16] but in all three of these areas that commitment is being tested by exercises of state power on behalf of another of liberalism's defining goals—equality.

Hate speech is regulated by the state on the theory that such expression denigrates the value and worth of its victims and the groups to which they belong.[17] Equality can also be found at work in the new assault on pornography by some feminists, who object to pornography not for religious or moral reasons but on the ground that it reduces women to sexual objects and eroticizes their domination.[18] In their view pornography leads to violence against women, including rape and domestic abuse, and beyond that to a pervasive pattern of social disadvantage, both in matters most intimate and in the public sphere. As with hate speech and pornography, the regulation of expenditures in electoral campaigns is also impelled by egalitarian considerations.[19] Some defend such regulation as a device to prevent corruption, but it can be understood in more generous terms—as a way of enhancing the power of the poor, putting them on a more nearly equal political footing with the rich, thus giving them a fair chance to advance their interests and enact measures that will improve their economic position.

Each generation tends to emphasize its uniqueness, and so one must be careful not to overstate the significance of the present moment. Regulations like the ones that so concern us today have been considered by the courts in earlier times. Yet I believe an important difference can be found in the depth of the legal system's commitment to equality today. Even in the 1960s, equality was but an aspiration, capable of moving the nation but still fighting to establish itself in the constitutional arena. Today, equality has another place altogether—it is one of the center beams of the legal order. It is architectonic.

When obscenity regulations were debated during the 1960s, consideration was of course given to the alleged power of sexually explicit films and magazines to arouse sexual drives and lead to rape. Little attention was given, however, to the effect that their perceived risk of rape might have on the day-to-day behavior of women, and to the impact pornography might have on the way women are viewed in society. In this formative period of obscenity doctrine, the egalitarian revolution in the law brought about by *Brown* had begun to move from blacks to the poor but had not yet reached women, not even at the level of ideology. True, a ban on gender discrimination was placed in the fair employment section of the Civil Rights Act of 1964, but as all the world knew, that addition was intended to sink the measure rather than to extend it.[20] Until the 1970s, the Civil Rights Act ban against employment discrimination based on sex was systematically slighted by the enforcement agencies, though in the last twenty years great efforts have been made to catch up. Today, gender equality has as strong a claim to the law's attention as does racial equality.

Many participants in the current debates readily acknowledge the pull of equality but refuse to capitulate to it. They honor the countervalue, yet resolve the conflict between liberty and equality in favor of liberty. The First Amendment should be first, they argue.[21] Such a position makes claim to the more classical conception of liberalism, and perhaps for that very reason has achieved a privileged position in current debates. It nevertheless seems vulnerable to me, because no reason is given for preferring liberty over equality—for preferring the First Amendment over the Fourteenth. The firstness of the First Amendment appears to be little more than an assertion or slogan. Those favoring liberty often refer to the role that free speech played in securing equality during the 1960s, suggesting that free and open debate is a precondition for achieving a true and substantive equality. But certainly the converse may also be true: that a truly democratic politics will not be achieved until conditions of equality have been fully satisfied.

In saying this, my intention is not to favor equality over liberty, to prefer the Fourteenth Amendment over the First Amendment, but only to acknowledge the difficulty, perhaps the impossibility, of discovering a method of choosing between these two values. The regulation of hate speech, pornography, and political expenditures forces the legal system to choose between transcendent commitments—liberty and equality— and yet the Constitution provides no guidance as to how that choice should be made. I therefore cannot agree with those partisans, including Catharine MacKinnon, who defend such regulations by simply asserting the priority of equality. They seem to be mirroring the error of the libertarians who assert the priority of speech.

I am also troubled by the attempt by Professor MacKinnon and others to work their way out of this conflict in ultimate values by defining liberty (in the form of free speech) out of the equation. MacKinnon argues that pornography is not speech at all but rather action, thus denying it the privileged status accorded to speech as an especially protected liberty.[22] In making this argument, she draws on a mode of analysis that was advanced in academic circles by Thomas Emerson at Yale[23] and that was once expounded by Justice Hugo Black.[24] I myself have doubts as to the usefulness of the speech/action distinction as a general First Amendment methodology because it masks all the hard judgments that the First Amendment requires. But even putting those more general concerns to one side, it seems to me that the distinction between action and speech is misplaced in this context.

Some forms of pornography—for example, movies and photographic magazines—may use women in the very process by which they are produced; the women who participate in such a productive process may well be engaged in action. Similarly, pornography may be one of the many causes or triggers of human action, including masturbation and violence against women. For that reason, pornography may be properly considered, as Catharine MacKinnon once said, as a mechanism of transmitting action from one domain to another. Still, I would insist, pornography itself is not reducible to either the action that produced it or the action that it causes but is a form of speech. Pornography is an expression of the creators and producers of the work and is most certainly part of the discourse by which the public understands itself and the world it confronts. A similar point can be made about hate speech, even when the speech in question might be characterized as "fighting words," "intimidation," or "harassment." Like pornography or for that matter much of art and literature, hate speech may appeal to our affective sentiments and be both the cause and the product of human action, but nonetheless is speech.

The effort to define the speech element out of hate speech and pornography defies common understanding of what is speech. An analogous argument was advanced in the context of campaign finance by Judge Skelly Wright in the 1970s, but in this case the argument has ordinary usage on its side.[25] His purpose was to justify regulating political expenditures against the argument that it violated the speech rights of the person making these expenditures. To put the regulations beyond the reach of the First Amendment, Judge Wright insisted that money is not speech. Once again, my inclination is to resist the easy way out and to claim, in defiance of common usage, that money is speech, or more accurately, that the act of spending money is as expressive an activity as parading and as important a method of advancing one's political values as seiling a book.

People sometimes give money to candidates or spend money on behalf of a cause as a way of communicating something about themselves or their beliefs. But even when political expenditures are purely instrumental and lack any expressive elements, they can still make claim to the First Amendment. The instruments needed to make a speaker's message effective and to bring the ideas to the public are protected by the First Amendment, though perhaps not as intensely as the speech itself. Account must be taken of the fact that the First Amendment protects not only the writing of books but also the facilities and institutions necessary to distribute books to the public.

IT MAY THUS seem that we have arrived at an impasse. We cannot avoid the problem posed by state regulation of hate speech, pornography, and campaign finance by simply defining speech out of the equation, and we have no principled way of resolving the conflict between liberty and equality. As a result, liberals have been divided, almost at war with themselves, some favoring liberty, some equality. We may have to live with this sorry state of affairs; but there may be another way of framing the issue that moves beyond this battle between transcendent values. Perhaps the regulations in question can be seen as themselves furthering, rather than limiting, freedom of speech

This understanding of what the state is seeking to accomplish would transform what at first seemed to be a conflict between liberty and equality into a conflict between liberty and liberty. This formulation would not make all disagreements go away, nor would it obviate the need for hard choices, but it would place those choices within a common matrix. It would make the controversy over regulation less a battle over ultimate values, a fruitless inquiry into whether the Fourteenth or the First Amendment comes first, and more a disagreement among strong-minded people working to achieve a common purpose: free speech.

In the history of free speech, the state has sometimes defended the regulation of speech in the name of liberty. For example, during the height of the Cold War, suppression of the

Communist Party and its leadership was often justified in terms of saving America from Stalinism.[26] The fear was that communist propaganda would, in time, be persuasive and would lead to the overthrow of the government or even the establishment of a totalitarian dictatorship. Characteristically, liberals responded that the remedy was more speech, not state regulation.

With pornography, hate speech, and campaign regulation, however, the alleged threat to freedom coming from speech is more direct and immediate. The claim is not that the speech will persuade listeners to act in a certain fashion—for instance, creating a new form of dictatorship or subjugating various disadvantaged groups in society. Rather, the fear is that the speech will make it impossible for these disadvantaged groups even to participate in the discussion. In this context, the classic remedy of more speech rings hollow. Those who are supposed to respond cannot.

It is asserted that hate speech tends to diminish the victims' sense of worth, thus impeding their full participation in many of the activities of civil society, including public debate. Even when these victims speak, their words lack authority; it is as though they said nothing. This silencing dynamic has also been attributed to pornography.[27] In this view, pornography reduces women to sexual objects, subordinating and silencing them. It impairs their credibility and makes them feel as though they have nothing to contribute to public discussion. In an even clearer case, unlimited political expenditures not only perpetuate the unequal distribution of wealth and put the poor at a disadvantage in the political arena but also may have the effect of silencing the poor. The rich may, for example, so dominate advertising space in the media and other public domains that the public will, in effect, hear only their message. As a result, the voice of the less affluent may simply be drowned out.[28]

In each of these cases the agency threatening speech values is not the state itself. Nor need it be. The call for state intervention is based not on the theory that the activity to be regulated is inherently a violation of the First Amendment (a claim that would require, as a purely technical matter, a showing of state action) but only on the theory that fostering full and open debate—making certain that the public hears all that it should—is a permissible end for the state. Even if the silencing dynamic is wrought solely by private hands—for example, by the person who hurls racial epithets or publishes pornography or uses superior economic resources to dominate political campaigns—there is ample basis for intervention. The state is merely exercising its police power to further a worthy public end, as it does when it enacts gun control or speed limit laws. In this case, the end happens to be a conception of democracy which requires that the speech of the powerful not drown out or impair the speech of the less powerful.

While the promotion of democratic values is a worthy—indeed, a compelling—public purpose, a question can be raised about the method by which that goal is pursued, specifically, whether it is consistent with the First Amendment. State regulation of the type we are considering might promote, under the best of assumptions, the speech rights of women, minorities, and the poor, but it necessarily diminishes the speech rights of racists, pornographers, and the rich. What gives the state the right to choose the speech rights of one group over the other? The answer to this question depends in large part on how we conceive the speech interests at stake, which in turn falls back on the distinction between libertarian and democratic conceptions of freedom.

If nothing more were involved than the self-expressive interests of each group, say the desire of the racist and the interest of the would-be victim each to speak his or her mind, then there would indeed be something arbitrary about the state's choosing one group over the other. I believe that something more is involved, however. The state is not trying to arbitrate between the self-expressive interests of the various groups but rather trying to establish essential preconditions for collective self-governance by making certain that all sides are presented to the public. If this could be accomplished by simply empowering the disadvantaged groups, the state's aim would be achieved. But our experience with affirmative action programs and the like has taught us that the matter is not so simple. Sometimes we must lower the voices of some in order to hear the voices of others.

In conceiving of state regulation of hate speech, pornography, and campaign finance in this manner, equality once again makes an appearance. But now the value is rooted in the First Amendment, not the Fourteenth Amendment. The concern is not simply with the social standing of the groups that might be injured by the speech whose regulation is contemplated. Rather, the concern is with the claims of those groups to a full and equal opportunity to participate in public debate—the claims of these groups to their right to free speech, as opposed to their right to equal protection. The state, moreover, is honoring those claims not because of their intrinsic value or to further their self-expressive interests but only as a way of furthering the democratic process. The state is trying to protect the interest of the audience—the citizenry at large—in hearing a full and open debate on issues of public importance.

RECONCEPTUALIZING the problems presented by hate speech, pornography, and campaign finance in this way might seem to accord easily with the traditional framework. It turns out that the countervalue we take seriously is not the bland public order, nor even the more alluring value of equality, but democracy itself. Indeed, one way of describing the situation is simply to say that now speech appears on both sides of the equation, as a value threatened by the regulation and as the countervalue furthered by it. But even this way of putting the matter radically understates the depth of the challenge we confront. Whereas the traditional framework rests upon the old liberal idea that the state is the natural enemy of freedom, now we are being asked to imagine the state as the friend of freedom.

Resistance to this reversal of the traditional dialectic of freedom is considerable. In part it is founded on an absolutist reading of the First Amendment as a bar to any state regulation of speech whatsoever.[29] This view of the First Amendment proclaims that "no law" means "no law," which is certainly true, but as Alexander Meiklejohn emphasized, what the First Amendment prohibits is laws abridging "the freedom of speech," not a freedom to speak.[30] The phrase "the freedom of speech" implies an organized and structured understanding of freedom, one that recognizes certain limits as to what should be included and excluded. This is the theory upon which speech regulation that aims to protect national security or public order is sometimes allowed; it should be equally available when the state is trying to preserve the fullness of debate. Indeed, the First Amendment should be more embracing of such regulation, since that regulation seeks to further the democratic values that underlie the First Amendment itself.

Although the Supreme Court has never taken kindly to absolutism in its reading of the First Amendment, over the course of the last twenty-five years it has increasingly fallen back on a principle that would seriously impair—though perhaps not altogether bar—the state's capacity to protect freedom. This is the principle of content neutrality, which prohibits the state from regulating speech on the basis of what is being said.

Starting with *Buckley v. Valeo*,[31] the Court has adamantly resisted mandatory limitations on political expenditures, even on the premise that these limitations prevent distortions of public debate. Time and again, the Court has declared that the First Amendment prohibits the state from restricting the voice of some so as to enhance the voice of others.[32] No justification was offered for this stance when it was initially proclaimed, but it seems to make appeal to the principle of content neutrality. In later cases, the Court explicitly linked the *Buckley* manifesto to that principle.[33]

On the issue of hate speech, the Court has not been so coy. In the 1992 decision in *R.A.V.* v. *St. Paul*—the so-called cross-burning case—the Court struck down the City of St. Paul's hate speech ordinance on the ground that it was not content neutral.[34] The Court assumed the ordinance proscribed only "fighting words," a category of expression that was within the power of the state to regulate or even suppress. Nonetheless, the Court invalidated the ordinance on the ground that it was partial. The "fighting words" of racists or sexists were prohibited but not those of individuals fighting racism or sexism. The state was favoring the tolerant over the intolerant. As Justice Scalia, writing for the majority, put it, "St. Paul has no authority to license one side to fight free style, while requiring the other to follow Marquis of Queensbury Rules."[35]

The Supreme Court has allowed the regulation of obscenity, provided that it stays within the bounds provided by the so-called *Miller* test,[36] but it has not yet had occasion to hear a case involving a regulation specifically structured to respond to feminist concerns regarding pornography. Its decision in the hate speech case, however, is indicative of how it might rule. Indeed, in justifying his conclusion in *R.A.V.*, Justice Scalia took as his first premise the view that a partial regulation of obscenity—a law that proscribed only obscenity that was critical of the city government—would be unconstitutional because it transgressed the rule requiring content neutrality.[37] Several years earlier a similar line of reasoning was used by Judge Frank Easterbrook in the Seventh Circuit Court of Appeals to strike down an Indianapolis ordinance that was aimed specifically at sexually explicit material that subordinated women.[38]

The principle of content neutrality bars the state from trying to control the people's choice among competing viewpoints by favoring or disfavoring one side in a debate. So understood, the principle has powerful appeal and can be profitably applied in many contexts. The abortion protests of the modern day provide one. It would violate democratic principles for the state to adopt a rule protecting parades and demonstrations by those who favor the right to abortion while clamping down on "pro-life" forces. On the other hand, content neutrality is not an end in itself and should not be reified. The principle responds to some underlying concern that the state might use its power to skew debate in order to advance particular outcomes, and this purpose should always be kept in mind. Accordingly, the principle should not be extended to situations like hate speech, pornography, and political expenditures, in which private parties are skewing debate and the state regulation promotes free and open debate. In those cases, the state may be disfavoring certain speakers—the cross-burner, the pornographer, or the big spender—and make judgments based on content, but arguably only to make certain that all sides are heard. The state is simply acting as a fair-minded parliamentarian, devoted to having all views presented.

In an earlier period, a number of First Amendment theorists, including Meiklejohn and Kalven—the architects of the liberal position—acknowledged that the state might sometimes have to act as a parliamentarian. But they assumed that the state could discharge that function simply by following Robert's Rules of Order: a predetermined method of proceeding based not on what was transpiring in debate but rather on some universal abstract principle like temporal priority.[39] Today, that conception is not sufficient. A parliamentarian must be sensitive to the limitations that resources—such as time and money—place on debate and might well have to say, "We have heard a lot from this side already. Perhaps others should get a chance to speak before we vote." A fair parliamentarian wants vigorous expression of views but is also sensitive to the excesses of advocacy and the impact of such excesses on the quality of debate. A fair parliamentarian might sometimes have to interrupt and say, "Can't you restrain yourself? You have been so abusive in the way you have put your point that many have withdrawn from the debate altogether."

Of course, any regulation of debate is likely to have an impact upon the public's final decision on a policy issue; any regulation of process is likely to affect outcome. Hearing two sides of a debate may well produce a decision different from that arrived at if only one side is heard. In that sense, the use of the principle of content neutrality to bar the regulation of hate speech, pornography, and campaign finance might seem similar to its use in the case of abortion protests, where state regulation would have the effect of favoring one side of the debate over the other. But there is a crucial difference.

When the state acts as a parliamentarian, its purpose is not to determine outcome, nor even to preserve public order (as it might be in the abortion protest case) but rather to ensure the robustness of public debate. Such a goal changes the analysis altogether. It is not that the enrichment of public debate is a more worthy goal than, say, the maintenance of public order, and thus more capable of excusing the impact that regulation has upon process and thus upon outcome. It may be that; but I am making a more fundamental point, namely, that the skewing of outcome by the enhancement of debate is no cause for concern. There is no wrong. What democracy exalts is not simply public choice but rather public choice made with full information and under suitable conditions of reflection. From democracy's perspective, we should not complain but rather applaud the fact that outcome was affected (and presumably improved) by full and open debate.

In speaking of the state as parliamentarian, Meiklejohn and Kalven treated society as though it were one gigantic town meeting. Recently, Professor Robert Post has insisted that such a view ultimately rests on antidemocratic premises, and he has criticized this way of understanding society.[40] According to Post, while actual town meetings take place against a background in which the participants agree to an agenda—sometimes implicitly or informally—no such assumptions can be made about civil society. In the constant conversation that is civil society, no one is ever out of order and no idea is ever beyond consideration. Civil society, he argued, can be thought of as a town meeting only if it too has an agenda, but the setting of an agenda would require a certain measure of dictatorial action by the state, what Post would regard as an exercise of its managerial powers, thus flouting the radical democratic—almost anarchic—possibilities that might be realized. Genuine democratic principles, according to Post, require that citizens set the public agenda and always be free to reset it.

The notion of a town meeting does indeed presuppose an agenda—there must be some standard of relevance—but agendas, either of actual town meetings or of the more metaphoric type, need not be set by the deliberate action of the participants nor imposed by an external force, such as the state. They can evolve more organically. In democratic societies there is always an agenda structuring public discussion—one week nuclear proliferation, the next health care—even though that agenda is not set by a particular agent or authority.

Society is more than a town meeting, and the state is significantly more than a parliamentarian. The state is also the embodiment of distinctive substantive policies, and those in control of its power have a vested interest in how debates are resolved. Sly politicians may say that they are regulating content in order to enrich public debate and to make certain that the public hears from all sides, but their purpose may, in fact, be to determine outcome or to further certain policies. This danger strikes me as particularly acute in the area of campaign finance, where incumbents may limit expenditures as a way of insulating themselves from the challenges of newcomers.

This danger must be confronted and dealt with directly. Those in charge of designing institutions should place the power to regulate content—to act as a parliamentarian—in agencies that are removed from the political fray. It is never a good idea to choose to chair a meeting someone who is keenly invested in one outcome. In addition, a heavy burden of scrutinizing the state's action should fall to the judiciary, especially because it stands apart from the political fray. In discharging this task, the judiciary should not look at the motive—stated or otherwise—for the action but must carefully determine what the overall effect of the state regulation is upon public debate. The court must ask itself: Will the regulation actually enhance the quality of debate, or will it have the opposite effect?

An inquiry into the impact of state intervention on the quality of debate is a difficult, somewhat tortuous exercise, and it is hard to know how it might come out in the three problems under consideration. I have grouped hate speech, pornography, and campaign finance together because of my theoretical interests—because I perceive them as presenting a similar challenge to received First Amendment doctrine—and not because I believe they all need to be resolved the same way. Although it is clear to me that, in grappling with these issues, the courts have erred in relying on a reified version of the principle of content neutrality, it is possible that even within a framework that conceives of the state as a parliamentarian and allows it sometimes to make content judgments, the courts might in fact conclude that the action of the state narrows debate and thus, in result alone, still come out the way they did.

That said, I do not believe that *Buckley v. Valeo,* invalidating the limitations on political expenditures, could be defended in these terms. The law in question in that case was enacted in the wake of Watergate and rested on a sober congressional judgment, amply supported by the evidence, about the distorting effect that unlimited political expenditures have on politics. But hate speech and pornography present more difficult issues. The silencing effect attributed to these two forms of speech depend on a more subtle psychological dynamic—one that disables or discredits a would-be speaker. In the specific case that comes before the court, the dynamic might not be present, or the chosen correctives might be clumsy, causing more distortions in public debate than they cure. The traditional remedy—more speech—might be far better. It is hard to be certain about these matters, especially when operating at this level of abstraction. Two points can be made about hate speech and pornography, however.

First, a failure of theory can lead to a failure of inquiry. Unable to appreciate or even acknowledge the possibility that they were confronted with a situation in which speech was both the threatened value and the countervalue, the courts in the St. Paul and Indianapolis cases invalidated the laws in question without even giving the state an opportunity to show how these forms of speech actually distort public debate or that the regulatory measures in question were appropriate correctives. The courts declared the laws invalid on their face.

Second, in arriving at their judgments, the courts in these

cases failed to give any weight to the Fourteenth Amendment version of the equality value, and this failure strikes me as an error. From the perspective of the First Amendment, we must attend to the silencing effect of hate speech and pornography on disadvantaged groups—how certain forms of speech violate the equal right to free speech of those groups; but this attention should not blind us to the impact that speech has upon the broader social status of those groups, that is, to the Fourteenth Amendment ramifications of those two forms of speech.

Even if the Fourteenth Amendment does not take priority over the First, that does not mean that the Fourteenth Amendment should be accorded no weight at all in the judicial calculus. Denying the priority of the Fourteenth Amendment does not obliterate it. It may have been hard to sustain the St. Paul hate speech ordinance and the Indianapolis pornography ordinance simply as speech-enhancing measures, but it may have been possible to compensate for the deficit of the First Amendment analysis and to tip the scale in favor of the state by broadening the focus of inquiry and taking into consideration the further cause of equality. All the countervalues should be honored.

A more powerful state creates dangers, there is no denying that; but the risk of these dangers materializing and an estimate of the harm that they will bring into being has to be weighed against the good that might be accomplished. We should never forget the potential of the state for oppression, never, but at the same time, we must contemplate the possibility that the state will use its considerable powers to promote goals that lie at the core of a democratic society—equality and perhaps free speech itself.

ART AND THE ACTIVIST STATE

2
—

In the history of political philosophy, the state has taken many forms. In the most familiar, the state acts in what might be called a regulatory manner, issuing commands and prohibitions and using the power at its disposal to enforce those directives. This is how the state typically acts in the criminal law—the state as policeman—and also in civil proceedings when it assesses damages and issues injunctions, and in a great deal of the administrative process when it issues cease-and-desist orders.

There is, however, another sphere of state activity of growing importance in the twentieth century, in which the state acts not as a regulator but as an allocator.[1] In this guise it awards licenses, builds and rents apartments, hires and fires people, buys books for libraries, funds and manages universities, and provides money for the arts. Some of these activities have no discernible connection to freedom of speech, but many do, either because subsidies are provided to speakers or because the award of benefits, such as jobs or passports, is tied to certain conditions affecting speech.

Most First Amendment scholars have focused on the regulatory function of the state and in that context have presented the Constitution as creating a shield around the street-corner speaker, protecting the individual citizen from the menacing arm of the policeman. They forged the First Amendment into an instrument of classical liberalism. In Chapter 1 I argued that this understanding of the First Amendment has to be radically adjusted to take account of the silencing effects of speech itself, when the state must act as a parliamentarian. In this chapter I will argue that the traditional view is even less adequate when confronting the state as allocator. Placing boundaries between state and speaker or conceiving of the First Amendment as a shield around the street-corner speaker has virtually no meaning in the allocative context, for in every allocation there is necessarily an interaction between the state and the citizen.

Some who have pursued classical liberalism to an extreme insist that the state not make grants to speakers at all. They would have a wall constructed between speech and the state, much like the wall separating religion and the state. This view may have some superficial appeal in discussing allocations to what some see as "frill-activities"—the favorite targets are public funding for the arts and public broadcasting—but becomes untenable when the question of public libraries and public education arises. In these cases, it is well understood that an abandonment of state funding would leave these activities, and thus our entire cultural and intellectual life, to the vicissitudes of the market or to the whims of those with enormous aggregations of wealth.

The more sensible approach is to start with public funding of cultural programs as an established fact of contemporary life and to use the First Amendment to protect against abuses of power in the administration of these programs. As a purely legal matter, all agree that the Constitution applies to state allocations as well as regulations. A grant by the state, like a criminal prosecution, is an act of the state and thus subject to the constraints of the First Amendment. Disagreement arises, however, over how the First Amendment applies and the degree to which it applies. Specifically, the question is whether the allocative state should be subjected to the same strict scrutiny as the regulatory one when it comes to speech.

THE QUESTION of formulating appropriate First Amendment standards for the activist state and its allocative processes has come up in many different settings in recent years, but never more urgently than in the controversy generated by the decision of the National Endowment for the Arts (NEA) to support an exhibition of Robert Mapplethorpe's work. Mapplethorpe was a New York photographer who died of AIDS in March 1989 at the age of 42. Shortly before his death a retrospective of his work was organized by the Institute of Contemporary Art of the University of Pennsylvania and funded by the NEA. Senator Jesse Helms of North Carolina, long a prominent figure in conservative circles, denounced a number of the photographs in the retrospective as "filth" and "trash" and complained about the use of federal funds to support the project.[2]

In its entirety, the Mapplethorpe retrospective consisted of 175 photographs.[3] Some, like the portraits of celebrity friends or the pictures of flowers, Helms apparently found inoffensive. The Senator's attack focused primarily on three groups of photographs of an entirely different nature. The first consisted of photographs of children of Mapplethorpe's friends. Included in this group was a photograph of a naked boy sitting on the back of a chair; there was also a photograph of a young girl sitting on a garden bench, with her dress raised. She was not wearing undergarments.

The second group of controversial photographs treated the

naked body as sculpture. The group included shots of a friend of Mapplethorpe's, a woman weight-lifter, but the ones that caused the greatest stir were of the male body and its various parts. One that particularly angered the Senator was entitled "Man in Polyester Suit." It is a photograph of a black man dressed in an inexpensive suit. The camera focuses on his torso, cropping the area beneath his knees and above his shoulders. His penis is exposed.

The third group of photographs proved the most objectionable. They depicted homosexual relationships. In one, two men, stripped to the waist, are embracing; in another, two men are kissing. Still others, part of the so-called "X" series, depicted homosexual activity that might be considered sado-masochistic: a man urinating into the mouth of another, a hand inserted in an anus. A good number of the photographs in the "X" series are, and are clearly intended to be, shocking and disturbing.

The NEA had given the Institute of Contemporary Art $30,000 to assemble the exhibition, and it was this tie between the state and the art world that generated the uproar. Senator Helms, in particular, thought it an outrage that public money was being spent for the Mapplethorpe exhibit. His protest led to the cancellation of the show at the Corcoran Gallery in Washington, D.C., just before it was scheduled to open late in the spring of 1989. The Senator's protest also led to two rounds of congressional legislation.

In the first, occurring in the fall of 1989, Congress added a rider to the NEA appropriation bill. This rider, referred to as the Helms Amendment, was intended to bar the NEA from using its funds to support art he thought comparable to Mapplethorpe's.[4] To describe the category of such art, Senator Helms used the term "obscene," a term that has special juridical significance. Starting in the late 1950s and continuing to this day, the Supreme Court has sought to place bounds on state regulation of sexually explicit material by propounding a constitutional definition of "obscenity." The prevailing definition, formulated in 1973 in *Miller v. California,* requires the prosecution to prove that the interdicted work taken as a whole appeals to a prurient interest in sex, depicts sexual conduct in a patently offensive manner, and lacks serious literary, artistic, political, or scientific value.[5]

At the time of Helms's initial attack, most constitutional lawyers assumed that the Mapplethorpe exhibition was protected from an obscenity prosecution under the *Miller* test. In the fall of 1990 this judgment was confirmed in Cincinnati, Ohio, where the Museum of Contemporary Art and its director were prosecuted under obscenity charges for presenting the exhibition.[6] A jury using the *Miller* test acquitted them, presumably because the exhibition had serious aesthetic and maybe even political value—as one expression of the insistent claim of the gay community, ravaged by AIDS, that "Silence = Death." Senator Helms made it clear, however, that his understanding of "obscenity" was different from the Supreme Court's and that the term, as used in the 1989 statute, was intended to be read more broadly than the *Miller* test permitted.

The Helms Amendment and the restriction it imposed on the NEA caused an enormous controversy in the art world and beyond. Some objected to the particular way the law was administered, specifically the agency's requirement that grant applicants sign a pledge to comply with the law.[7] Parallels were drawn to the loyalty oaths of the McCarthy period. Another objection was tied more to the specific terms of the law and stemmed from the fact that the Helms Amendment did not confine itself to the *Miller* test for obscenity. In truth, however, there was no need for the law to do so. Obscenity statutes are allowed to stand even though they in fact contain no definition of obscenity or define obscenity more broadly than the *Miller* test does, for that test operates only as a limitation in the applicability of the law. Overreaching can generally be cured by the courts on a case-by-case basis by confining a law to its constitutionally permissible limits; this approach could have been applied to the Helms Amendment, assuming—as most critics did—that the restrictions it imposed on eligibility for NEA funding would have been subject to the same constitutional standards as an obscenity prosecution.

In any event, the Helms Amendment expired at the end of the fiscal year, along with the appropriations bill to which it was attached. Then, in the fall of 1990, shortly after the Cincinnati verdict, Congress enacted a new statute for the NEA, the one that governs today.[8] In terms of administrative practice, the 1990 statute sought to focus more responsibility on the chairperson for selection of recipients. It contemplates continued use of peer review panels in awarding grants but assumes that those panels will recommend more applicants than can be funded and that the final choice for the NEA grants would be the responsibility of the chairperson. Even more significant were the changes the 1990 statute introduced in the standards to be used in granting awards, though in this instance the statute moved in two different directions.

Like the Helms Amendment, the 1990 statute bars the NEA from funding obscene works and thus establishes nonobscenity as a condition of eligibility. But in contrast to Helms's measure, the concept of obscenity is tied directly and explicitly to the juridical definition of the term in *Miller*. In a similar spirit, the 1990 statute provides that the judgment whether a work or project meets the definition of obscenity is to be left to the courts. No project can be deemed ineligible for NEA funding on the ground that it is obscene unless and until a court concludes that it is. (Provision is made for recoupment by the

NEA if such a determination is made after the award of a grant.)

Although the 1990 statute brought the law into conformity with the *Miller* test in setting eligibility standards, it lessened the standards to govern what might be termed the competitive phase of the application process, that is, when the agency chooses among eligible applicants. For the competitive phase, the 1990 statute introduced a new term, "decency." Along with artistic merit or excellence, decency became one of the bases for choosing among eligible applicants. Artistic excellence is a plus factor, indecency a negative one. The 1990 statute provides that "artistic excellence and artistic merit are the criteria by which applicants are judged, taking into consideration general standards of decency and respect for the diverse beliefs and values of the American public."[9]

The 1990 statute thereby took the NEA, to borrow another Kalven expression,[10] out from under the Constitution, at least partially. Although the law holds the NEA to First Amendment standards in eligibility determination, it permits wider latitude in the competitive phase. The statute allows—indeed, requires—the chairperson to deny grants to projects on the ground that they offend "general standards of decency." Presumably this ground could be used to deny funding to projects like the Mapplethorpe retrospective, and if that happened the question posed would be whether such action violates the First Amendment and the guarantee of freedom of speech. Against the background of the failed Cincinnati prosecution, which could be taken to establish that Mapplethorpe's work is constitutionally protected from a criminal prosecution for obscenity, the precise question would be whether the NEA should be allowed powers denied the policeman or, to use my initial formulation, whether the allocative state should be held to the same First Amendment standards as the regulatory one.

In approaching the question, I start with the assumption that, in terms of the First Amendment, the public consequences of the regulatory and allocative actions of the state are roughly the same. The great danger to First Amendment values posed by the Cincinnati prosecution inhered in its potential impact on access or exposure of the citizenry to the work of Mapplethorpe. It threatened to keep the Mapplethorpe exhibit from the public. Denial of NEA funding could have the same effect. The institution that applied to the NEA to assemble the exhibition may have lacked the funds to make the endeavor economically viable on its own, and rejection of its application might well have kept the exhibition from the public. Admittedly, criminal prosecution may stigmatize an individual artist, destroy his or her reputation, or even result in imprisonment. But in fact criminal prosecutions for obscenity rarely lead to imprisonment, and denying an artist or a curator a grant because a work is indecent may have the same impact on reputation as a criminal prosecution. In terms of the hardship imposed on individual artists, curators, or even institutions, is there really any difference between fining the Cincinnati museum $2,000 for displaying the Mapplethorpe exhibition and denying the Institute of Contemporary Art the funds—say $30,000—needed to assemble the exhibit? I think not.

It is hard to offer general conclusions with such inherently pragmatic judgments, however. So let us assume for the moment that regulatory action (in the form of a criminal prosecution) creates unique hardships. Also, let us assume that a criminal conviction on obscenity grounds creates a greater stigma than denial of funds on decency grounds. It is not clear, however, what follows from these premises. The special hardships may trigger the procedural safeguards of the Fifth and Sixth Amendments, but I believe they are irrelevant to the constitutional interests protected and promoted by the First

ART AND THE ACTIVIST STATE

Amendment. This is true whether we consider the democratic value that the First Amendment seeks to advance (the promotion of robust public debate) or the libertarian one (protection of the individual's interest in self-expression). The stigma or special hardship of the criminal prosecution enters into the analysis of the First Amendment issue only insofar as it enhances the severity of the criminal sanction, whether it be imprisonment or a fine. Even then, great economic need might give a denial of funding similar force.

There is, however, one essential difference between the regulatory and allocative forms of action: A certain measure of silencing is inevitable in the allocative context. This silencing effect arises from the scarcity of resources—the simple fact that the money to be disbursed by the NEA is always likely to fall short of the total number of grant requests. An award given to one applicant will necessarily be denied to another and, as a result, the action of the state will simultaneously have both speech-enhancing and speech-restricting qualities. The speech of the applicant who gets the award will be enhanced, but that of the one who was denied the grant will be curbed. Of course, the applicants who are denied the grant are still "free" to pursue the project on their own, but once it is assumed that the subsidies have a productive function—that they bring forth art that otherwise would not exist—that freedom is largely formal. Applicants denied the grant may well lack the resources needed to bring their art into being, and to that extent their expression will be frustrated in the same way that the expression of artists who receive the grant is furthered.

In the regulatory context no such scarcity of resources is present and the decision of the state does not have this double-edged quality. A decision by the policeman to arrest the street-corner speaker will result in a loss of speech, but a decision by a the policeman to stand back ordinarily will not have that effect. Putting aside the special problems discussed in the previous chapter, when the silencing effect comes from the speech itself, or the problem to be considered in the next chapter, when a heckler threatens the street-corner speaker, the decision of the policeman not to make an arrest will produce more speech. But in the allocative context, an award of a grant will—thanks to scarcity—limit speech just as much as it enhances it.

To be precise, scarcity is not always at work in allocations. Specifically, it is not present at the eligibility stage of the allocative process since at that point there is no need to choose among applicants. There can always be more applicants declared eligible than there are funds. For that reason, eligibility determinations can be treated in much the same way as regulatory actions; they can be governed, as the 1990 statute recognizes but Helms disputed, by the *Miller* test. But at the competitive phase, the *Miller* test is of no use, for choices still have to be made among a large number of applicants, all of whom can be presumed to have passed the obscenity test. Going further, a question may be raised as to whether the First Amendment has anything at all to say about choices at the competitive stage. True, the state in the form of the NEA is acting, but no matter what the NEA chooses, by the very act of selecting one applicant over another it will simultaneously both discourage and encourage speech.

The First Amendment would indeed be indifferent to the NEA's choice if that provision were conceived, as some insist, simply as a protection of the self-expressive interests of individual artists and curators. An artist denied an award would have his or her interest in self-expression frustrated, but the one who got the award would have that very same interest furthered. There would be, it seems, no constitutional basis for questioning the selection by the NEA of one applicant over another.

Taken in isolation, each applicant has an equal interest in self-expression. A constitutional indifference would also arise if the more compelling theory of the First Amendment—the public debate rationale—were conceived in purely quantitative terms: The shrinkage of public debate due to the denial of one applicant would be fully compensated by the grant of the very same funds to another artist or curator.

However, if the public debate rationale can be understood to have not just a quantitative but also a qualitative dimension—if the First Amendment can be viewed as a mechanism for protecting the robustness of public debate, for exposing the public to diverse and conflicting viewpoints on issues of public importance—then there is reason to be concerned with the NEA's allocative decisions at the competitive phase. Some choices may enrich public understanding while others may impoverish it.

Imagine that in making allocations at the competitive phase the chairperson were directed to take into consideration whether or not the project furthered so-called family values or, more specifically, orthodox understandings of sexuality. A project that portrayed homosexuality sympathetically would be disfavored, while one that reinforced heterosexuality would be favored. This directive would have the effect of constricting public discourse—advantaging traditional views of sexuality while further marginalizing alternative views; one view, and only one view, would be pushed. The NEA could be rightly charged with reinforcing an orthodoxy and thus betraying one of the fundamental principles of the First Amendment. The mere fact that a choice somehow had to be made between competing artistic projects, and that in the competitive phase some silencing effect was inevitable, would not take the statutory directive and the chairperson's action under it outside the scope of the First Amendment.

In this imagined case, we can condemn the statutory criterion altogether because it would almost certainly lead to an impoverishment of what I have referred to as public debate. It would make debate entirely lopsided. It is harder, however, to make such blanket judgments about a criterion actually used in the 1990 NEA statute—decency. Suppose that there are two projects that challenge orthodox views about sexuality, one executed in a manner more in accord with general standards of decency than the other. Or suppose there is a project that promotes an orthodox view of sexuality or the prevailing distribution of wealth but does so in a way that deeply offends general standards of decency. In these cases, a proper concern for First Amendment values would not necessarily preclude the NEA chairperson from taking decency into account. One must make certain that the decency criterion is not being used to disfavor the unorthodox, and one should acknowledge that it might have a tendency in that direction, but it is hard to rule out the criterion altogether. As with the *Miller* test, case-by-case judgments would be needed in this instance, to see whether the decency criterion is being applied or understood in such a way as to systematically disadvantage certain perspectives and thus to impoverish public debate.

A gap between regulatory and allocative action is thereby created when it comes to the competitive phase and use of the decency criterion. The policeman cannot arrest the street-corner speaker simply because that speaker is offending general standards of decency; yet the chairperson of the NEA may select one speaker or applicant over another because the preferred project does less violence to general standards of decency. There is no need to prove that the "speech" appeals a to prurient interest in sex or is patently offensive in its depiction of sexual activity—the requirements for an obscenity prosecution, at least under established doctrine. On the other hand, this gap between regulatory and allocative action is a limited one. Although the decency criterion may be appropriately used, for example, as a tie-breaker between two projects of equal artistic merit, it should never be employed in a way that impairs the robustness of public debate or cuts the public off from unorthodox ideas—as a denial to Mapplethorpe might have done. Such a use of the decency criterion might be permitted by the 1990 statute but not by the Constitution. The Constitution prohibits such allocations and, in thus confining the applicability of the statute, works in much the same way as does in the obscenity area.

An even more complex theoretical issue is presented by the other allocative criterion set forth in the 1990 statute—artistic merit.[11] Many of those who fought Senator Helms in the Mapplethorpe controversy insisted that the First Amendment be read as requiring that NEA judgments be based exclusively on artistic merit. This restriction would have the effect of precluding the use of the decency criterion (or one of its cognates), which many thought would be used as a tool for weeding out the unorthodox. But it would also have the effect of making judgments based on artistic merit immune from constitutional scrutiny. Once it was ascertained that the NEA based its judgment solely on artistic merit, there would be no further basis for inquiry.

To some extent, those who took this position were moved by the peculiarities of the Mapplethorpe situation. The exhibition challenged an orthodoxy; it brought into view the lives and practices of a marginalized group, revealing that group's understanding of the erotic and boldly confronting society with the consequences of its intolerance—for example, the self-loathing depicted in the "X" series. But, as was clearly demonstrated in the Cincinnati trial, the exhibition was also an aesthetic achievement of some note. Accordingly, funding for the Mapplethorpe exhibition could be seen as furthering both artistic and democratic values, and it was natural for those who resisted Helms to assume, as a purely instrumental matter, that reliance on artistic excellence as a selection criterion would adequately protect democratic values. In my view, however, it was wrong to generalize from the Mapplethorpe exhibition and presume that these two values will always be in harmony. In fact, sometimes they may diverge: "good art" may undermine democratic values, while "bad art" may further them.

Another school raced to equate freedom of speech and artistic excellence, or more precisely, to make the latter the standard of the first, not because they mistook the Mapplethorpe case for the general situation but rather because they were searching for a principled basis for their reaction to Senator Helms. They hoped to "depoliticize" the NEA and to use artistic excellence as a "neutral" ground for the NEA to stand upon. But if we have learned anything from our encounter with race issues over the last three decades, it is that the use of so-called meritocratic criteria—in the race context, performance on standardized tests; here, artistic excellence—will not necessarily ensure neutrality.[12]

In the speech context, neutrality means that the state does not lend itself to one side of a debate over another. The people, not the state, should choose among competing viewpoints, and their choice should not be manipulated by the state by skewing public debate in some special way. Yet this objective cannot be achieved by making the use of a seemingly neutral criterion the touchstone of constitutionality. To see why, imagine the state making an allocation on the basis of a criterion that is in no way neutral: The state gives money to a certain project for the purpose of helping the side represented by that project win the debate. Also assume, however, that as it turns out the allocation has no such effect. The side preferred by the state actually gets no advantage. In a case like this, the state did not use a neutral criterion, but since there was no discernible impact on public debate from the perspective of the First Amendment and the values it seems to further, I see little reason to be concerned. Alternatively, we can imagine a situation in which a state official strives to be neutral, intending to give funds to the best art, regardless of its impact on public debate, yet the allocative decision has the effect of slanting the debate in favor of one side. Here there would be a breach of neutrality and good reason for the law to be concerned. We must thus look to the effects of an allocation, not its underlying basis or motive.

Some allocative criteria, including arguably the "family values" one I mentioned earlier, might be ruled out from the beginning, but that is only because of a prediction of its likely effect. No such sweeping judgment could be made about artistic excellence, and thus we are remitted to making case-by-case judgments. The effect of using artistic excellence will vary from situation to situation, depending on the structure of public discourse, the range of available projects, and the specific content given to the idea of artistic excellence. In this respect, artistic excellence is much like the decency criterion. Artistic excellence appears more innocent, or more appropriate for the NEA, but we must always be sensitive to the real-world consequences of using that criterion. The facial innocence of an allocative criterion does not ensure the kind of neutrality that the First Amendment demands.

Every NEA allocation will have an effect on public debate, so what is needed to judge such allocations is some standard to distinguish pernicious effects from harmless ones. I believe that standard can be found in the view of the First Amendment that sees it as a protection of collective self-determination: to ensure the fullness and richness of public debate. The application of a seemingly neutral criterion, whether it be artistic excellence or even decency, becomes a source of concern whenever it systematically keeps opinions from the public to which they should be exposed in order to govern themselves or to choose the kinds of lives they wish to live. Admittedly, presenting the public with diverse and conflicting viewpoints will itself have an impact on outcome, and in that limited sense is not neutral as to outcome, but as I explained in the last chapter, that does not threaten First Amendment values. Presenting two sides of an argument, instead of one alone, may produce a different outcome. But from democracy's perspective, that should not be viewed as a breach of the state's duty of neutrality, properly understood.

In sum, under the scheme I propose, in the administration of the competitive phase the NEA remains free to choose among eligible applicants as the 1990 statute directs, on considerations of artistic merit and decency, but it is also under a constitutional obligation, derived from the First Amendment, to make certain that these criteria are not applied in such a way as to impoverish public debate by systematically disfavoring views the public needs for self-governance. The First Amendment does not invalidate the statutory criteria but requires that they be supplemented. It triangulates the allocative process. The First Amendment requires the NEA chairperson to think not just of artistic excellence and decency but also of the public's right to know.

In this respect, the burden on the NEA and its chairperson is analogous to that shouldered by many other allocative agencies, including university admissions officers. Admissions officers use multiple and vague criteria. They must give substantive content to each criterion, and then decide the relative weight that should be given to each. Their institution is committed to providing education, not ensuring the civic health of the republic or furthering its egalitarian aspirations. Yet these officers must make certain that the criteria typically used for admissions—academic excellence, leadership potential, alumni relationship—do not have the effect of systematically excluding certain disadvantaged groups. Sometimes that requires reconsidering or reinterpreting the once-standard criteria; in other instances, it calls for modifying or lessening their role in the selection process.

This reference to the experience of university admissions may indicate that the duty placed on the NEA by the First Amendment is not as unusual as it first seems, that it is well in accord with administrative practices found throughout society and that it is within the capacities of the agency. It may also point to a legal dilemma that lies slightly beneath the surface: The NEA may violate the law by trying to honor it. Even when the NEA considers the impact that the criteria set forth in the statute have upon the robustness of debate, some unorthodox ideas inevitably will be privileged, once again thanks to the scarcity factor. There are simply not enough funds to go to every unorthodox idea. The NEA administrator might give a plus to art that enhances the public's understanding of homosexuality but not to Nazi art or art that promulgates flat-earth theories. The administrator must then worry whether the privileging of one set of unorthodox ideas over another violates the First Amendment. I do not believe that it necessarily does, any more than a university privileging one disadvantaged group over the other—say, African Americans as opposed to Appalachians or South Asians—necessarily entails a violation of the Fourteenth Amendment.[13] It all depends on the justification for the privileging.

The choice among the unorthodox should not turn on the administrator's judgment about the goodness or badness of the ideas being advanced or whether the administrator thinks they have merit. This would violate the democratic aspiration of the First Amendment, which is to leave judgments as to the merits of various ideas to the people. There are a number of other factors that may be properly considered, however. Some might actually account for the widely shared view that the

Mapplethorpe exhibition was entitled to NEA funding, more so than other exercises in the unorthodox, while other factors may push in the opposite direction.

One factor that should be considered concerns the *relative degree of exclusion*. Just as some minority groups may be more disadvantaged than others, some unorthodox ideas may be more hidden from public view than others. Arguably, all unorthodox ideas have claim under the First Amendment to public funding, but perhaps those most unavailable to the public have the greatest claim. Today, and certainly after the movie *Philadelphia*, the plight of the gay community and the threat of AIDS are well known. But this was not so in 1989, making the case for funding the Mapplethorpe exhibition then all the more urgent.

In addition, some consideration should be given to *financial need*. The democratic theory of the First Amendment exalts the public's right to know and to be informed, and that right may be adequately satisfied without the assistance of public funding, say through the art market or other commercial outlets, such as television or movies. Today, Mapplethorpe's work enjoys great economic success and presents a weak First Amendment claim for funding. This may not have been the case at the time of the initial application for NEA funding and before the Helms attack.

The NEA administrator must also have some understanding of the choices and questions that are presently on the *public agenda*. Although debate should not be confined to the concerns of the moment, it nonetheless seems proper in the award of public funds to privilege those projects that illuminate issues that are of immediate concern to the nation. In the late 1980s the AIDS crisis confronted America in the starkest fashion and provoked urgent questions regarding the scope and direction of publicly funded medical research. To address those issues the public—represented by the casual museum visitor—needed an understanding of the lives and practices of the gay community, so long hidden from view.

Finally, the NEA administrator should consider a dynamic explored in the last chapter: the *silencing potential* of speech. The First Amendment and a proper regard for the needs of public debate requires that the NEA administrator attend to the impact the statutory criteria have upon the unorthodox, but it would be a sad irony for the administrator choosing among unorthodox projects to ignore the impact the expressions of certain unorthodox ideas have upon these very same values. A distinction should therefore be drawn between projects that, for example, resort to hate speech and the Mapplethorpe exhibition, which dealt explicitly with questions of sexuality but which did not, as far as I can tell, have the effect of silencing anyone. If anything, it became a source of empowerment for the members of the gay community.

SHALL THE allocative state be held to the same high standards as the regulatory one? Using the Mapplethorpe exhibition and the controversy it generated as something of a testing ground, I have tried to show why that question should be answered in the affirmative and why the courts should be acutely sensitive to the impact state allocations have on the robustness of public debate. In arguing for this unitary standard, I drew upon a wide body of law, some from equal protection as well as free speech, and also compared the arts administrator and the university admissions officer, each trying to further constitutional goals of considerable magnitude. In 1991, however, soon after the second round of congressional legislation on the NEA, the Supreme Court handed down a decision that moved the law in the opposite direction. That case—*Rust v. Sullivan*[14]—did not involve public funding of the arts but rather federally funded abortion clinics. Yet the First Amendment challenge to the administration of that program was dismissed with such a vengeance and with such force as to virtually free all state allocations, including those for the arts, from the strictures of the First Amendment. In much the style of classical liberalism, the Court in *Rust* placed state allocations on an entirely different constitutional plane than state regulations.

The Court in *Rust* was divided five to four, and the majority opinion was written by Chief Justice Rehnquist. The majority upheld an executive regulation that prohibited those working for federally funded family planning clinics from giving patients information on how to obtain abortions and, more significantly for First Amendment purposes, from advocating on behalf of abortion in the course of their employment. Employees could advocate against abortion but not for it. In other words, the state was using the public purse to favor one side in the most heated debate of our time.

Writing for the Court, Rehnquist stressed the unique method of state intervention that was involved: The state was acting not as a policeman but as an allocator, deciding what could be done with its funds. Not only did he free allocations from the rule against content judgments by the state—a fair and proper ruling, since state allocations necessarily entail such judgments, unless of course we resort to randomized distributions—but also, and more significantly, he freed allocations from the principle lying behind the rule against content regulations, specifically the obligation of the state to maintain free and open debate on issues of public importance. In dismissing the First Amendment claim in *Rust,* the Chief Justice seemed altogether indifferent to the effects allocative decisions might have upon the robustness of public debate.

To some extent, this indifference is the natural result of Rehnquist's attachment to a theory of the First Amendment that sees it more as a protection of the individual interest in self-expression than of society's interest in full and open debate.

This has been one of the organizing principles of Rehnquist's First Amendment jurisprudence, as fully controlling in the regulatory context as in the allocative one. In the regulatory context, this theory has its problems, and even more so in the allocative one. It deprives the courts of any basis for scrutinizing allocative decisions, since of necessity they involve favoring one individual over another.

Yet there seems to be something deeper and perhaps more enticing lying at the base of *Rust v. Sullivan*—a conception of subsidies as gifts, a repeated emphasis on the entirely optional and discretionary nature of the state's decision to grant subsidies in the first place.[15] According to the Chief Justice, we should be thankful for what the state has graciously given us and thus we should accept whatever limits the state wishes to impose, however offensive they may be. To use a phrase Rehnquist brought to the law earlier, we "must take the bitter with the sweet."[16]

In my view, the Constitution is more demanding than this canon of etiquette suggests. We should not be satisfied with just *any* subsidy program on the premise that it is better than none. A program with certain limits built into it—no advocacy of unorthodox ideas, for example—would have the effect of skewing public debate by reinforcing the prevailing orthodoxy and thus of undermining the workings of democracy. Perhaps the state need not provide megaphones to anyone, but once it decides to do so, it cannot give them out in such a way as to perpetuate an orthodoxy.

Oddly enough, Rehnquist himself paid lip-service to this idea in *Rust;* he acknowledged that even in the allocative context, government cannot *aim* at the suppression of dangerous ideas.[17] He never explained, however, why the concern need only be with the aims or motives of the state and need not extend to the effects of state allocations upon public debate. In the context of *Rust,* furthermore, it seems hard to argue that the motive was anything other than to suppress an idea that those in charge of the state apparatus considered dangerous or objectionable.

Often subsidies are far, far more than gifts, despite what Justice Rehnquist may think. Sometimes they seek to advance interests of a fundamental, indeed of a constitutional, nature. Admittedly, even when that is the case, a party may not be able to sue the government to force the establishment of such a program because of difficulties in structuring the remedy, for example, or in setting the precise level of funding. In that sense, the establishment of the subsidy program may not be obligatory,[18] but it may be more than merely permissible. It may be constitutionally *favored*—an intermediate category lying between the permissible and the obligatory—and by virtue of this status entitled to the same degree of scrutiny as that given to regulatory programs of the state. As a constitutionally favored activity, a subsidy program cannot be viewed as entirely discretionary.

In my view, the programs of the NEA enjoy such a privileged status. NEA grants are not simple gratuities, sops for the art world. Rather, they free art from strict dependence on the market or privately controlled wealth and thus make an important contribution to furthering the value that underlies the First Amendment: our right and duty to govern ourselves reflectively and deliberately. NEA grants, therefore, should be deemed constitutionally favored, not simply permitted, and deserve something more than the judicial indifference manifested in *Rust*. Judges must come to understand that in establishing the NEA, Congress was seeking to further the public's right to know and that judicial scrutiny of the program would be not an ungracious response to a gift—an effort to separate the bitter from the sweet—but only an effort to make certain that the higher ambitions of the program are fulfilled.

Such a view, of course, challenges the tenets of classical liberalism, which puts the state at war with liberty and conceives of the First Amendment as little more than a mechanism to stay the hand of the policeman. But, as I have argued, in the case of subsidy programs the First Amendment can become an instrument of democratic self-government, serving as both the rationale of the program and the ground for scrutinizing the way it is administered. This is the lesson that emerges from our analysis of the Mapplethorpe controversy, and it may well extend beyond public funding of the arts to a wide variety of allocative programs—the public libraries, public schools, state universities, and public broadcasting—that perform similar functions in our society and warrant the same constitutionally favored status as the NEA.

There may even be important implications for allocative programs that have no discernible connection to speech, such as those that provide medical or housing assistance to the poor. Such non-speech-related programs may not advance First Amendment interests but do give life to other constitutional provisions, such as the Fourteenth Amendment, and might also be viewed as more than merely permissible. They, too, might be constitutionally favored and for that reason subject to the same evaluative standards as their regulatory counterparts. The First Amendment is generally viewed as the most libertarian of all constitutional provisions, the constitutional breeding ground for state minimalism. So if we can see that the NEA and other speech-subsidy programs are consistent with, indeed favored by, the First Amendment, then the constitutional foundation for rejecting the classical liberal ideal of the minimal state and embracing state activism in meeting all manner of needs will have been placed on the most secure footing.

THE DEMOCRATIC MISSION OF THE PRESS

3

Democracy is an exercise in collective self-governance, requiring that state officials be chosen by the people and that the state be responsive to the desires and interests of the people. In exercising this sovereign prerogative, citizens depend upon a number of institutions to inform them about the positions of various contenders for office and to report and evaluate the ongoing policies and practices of government. In modern society the organized press, including television, is perhaps the principal institution that performs this function, and in order to discharge these democratic responsibilities the press needs a certain measure of autonomy from the state.

One form of autonomy is economic. For more than two hundred years newspapers in the United States have been privately owned, and we have had private ownership of radio and television ever since those technologies became available. The press is not economically dependent on the state for funds, nor are state officials able to manipulate the press by hiring and firing journalists or broadcasters.

A second form of autonomy is juridical. There is a body of judicial doctrine that places limits on the state's capacity to silence its critics, in particular the press, by criminal and civil proceedings. This autonomy has emerged from many sources, the most important of which is the 1964 decision of the Supreme Court in *New York Times v. Sullivan*,[1] the subject of Anthony Lewis's recent celebratory book.[2] In that case, the Supreme Court construed the First Amendment to mean that the press cannot be criminally prosecuted for libeling the state considered as an abstract entity. The Court also limited the power of public officials to recover damages in defamation actions, holding that public officials cannot recover for false statements bearing on their performance of their duties unless they prove that those statements were published or broadcast with knowledge or reckless disregard of their falsity.

This juridical autonomy reinforces the economic autonomy of the press. Both keep the state at bay and have been nourished by our governing ideologies, capitalism and liberalism. Orthodox capitalism envisions a strict separation of state and economy and demands that state interference with entrepreneurial activity be kept to a minimum.[3] Similarly, classical liberalism imagines the state as the natural enemy of freedom and insists that state intervention in people's lives be limited. These two ideologies have long had a powerful, almost captivating, call upon the American soul, and now endow the economic and juridical autonomy enjoyed by the press with a certain mystique. It is hard to imagine the press discharging its democratic responsibilities without a strong measure of autonomy. In the 1960s, however, a number of lawyers began to wonder aloud whether democracy required something more. Might the state have a role in furthering the democratic mission of the press?

THESE musings did not come out of thin air. Indeed, they reflected a deeper, more complex understanding of why autonomy was conferred on the press in the first place. *New York Times Co. v. Sullivan* spoke of a national commitment to a debate on issues of public importance that is "uninhibited, robust, and wide-open"[4]—a phrase used many times in this book, even more so in the annals of the Supreme Court—and it was this statement of the guiding purpose of the First Amendment that led many to wonder whether the state might have more of a role to play in regulating the press than had been previously allowed. The economic and juridical autonomy of the press secured for it a measure of independence from the state, but there were other forces—above all, the market—that constrained the press in its coverage of public issues and that might cause it to fail in discharging its duty of keeping the public informed.

A privately owned press is free of economic control by the state, which is, of course, to the good, but it is constrained by the economic structure within which it is embedded. Like other entrepreneurs, owners of newspapers or television and radio stations seek to maximize revenue and minimize costs. In short, they wish to make a profit, and their decisions on what to report and how to report it are largely determined by this desire. The market, bearing down on the press, may cause it to be shy in its criticism of the government or of certain candidates for office, when the government policies or the candidates' positions favor the economic interests of the press. In other instances, the influence may be more subtle: A simple desire to maximize profits may lead the press to slight issues that should be aired but will not be because they will not generate the desired revenue. To counteract the effects of the market and free the press from some of its constraints, a number of theorists turned to the state.

Some of those who envisioned a larger role for the state spoke of "monopoly power." They invoked statistics about the number of cities in America without newspapers or with only one newspaper—a shockingly high number—and referred to the privileged position of the three major networks in capturing viewers' attention.[5] I always found this way of analyzing the issue unconvincing, not because I saw cable or the new information technologies on the horizon but rather because those who couched their arguments in terms of monopoly power conceived of the market too narrowly. For constitutional purposes, the relevant market is an informational one, the domain from which the public finds out about the world that lies beyond its immediate experience. The relevant market cannot be defined medium-by-medium but must embrace newspapers, radio, television, magazines, books, and even movies as a unitary whole. In that market, there are dominant or leading forces that shape public opinion, but there is no monopoly.

While some turned to the state as a mechanism for curbing monopoly power—as a mechanism for perfecting the market—others had a broader, more political or constitutional purpose in mind: to fulfill the preconditions of democratic self-governance. Within this school, however, a crucial distinction needs to be made between two different factions—populists and perfectionists.[6] The populists complained about a gap between market-determined speech (the coverage and reportage that would result from the workings of a competitive market) and democratically determined speech (the coverage and reportage that would be chosen by a people assembled in some imagined democratic convention). The populists acknowledged that competition and the profit motive drive publishers and broadcasters to make their products attractive to the public, but pointed to a number of factors that make the market an imperfect reflection of what the people want.

One was costs. The pursuit of profits pushes media executives not only to maximize revenue but also to minimize costs, a dynamic that may lead them to slight high-cost news gathering activities and to rely instead on reruns of *I Love Lucy*. A second distortion arises from advertising, the method typically used by the privately owned press to generate revenue. Media corporations must be careful to make certain that the content of their broadcasts or newspapers enhances rather than impedes sales of the advertised products. Political controversy is not a good way to sell soap. Third, dependence on advertising necessarily leads publishers and broadcasters to discriminate among potential readers and viewers in determining what they present and how they will present it. Those driven by market pressures seek to attract particular "target audiences," not the public in general. These audiences are defined in terms of their purchasing power and susceptibility to advertising, hardly the democratic norm of one person, one vote. Finally, the populists decried the absence of collective deliberation in a market-driven system. People register their preferences in a market through highly individualized transactions, for example, through the purchase of a newspaper on the way home from work or the selection of a television station in the privacy of their home. The choices that they make in such settings might well be different from those that would be made after collectively discussing and debating all the options.

Others concerned with the constitutional adequacy of the market—the perfectionists—accepted the populist critique of the market but saw state intervention in more abstract terms. Their goal was not to offer what the people would want in some imagined democratic assembly but rather to achieve an objective ideal: apprising the people of the issues before them, providing them with the necessary information, and presenting them with the conflicting positions. The hope, to use a phrase from an early press case, was to have "the widest possible dissemination of information from diverse and antagonistic sources."[7] The perfectionists admitted that the people might not want this kind of coverage, that they might prefer sex and violence to analysis of public issues; nonetheless the perfectionists felt that the press should be encouraged, induced, or maybe even required to provide the information that people need to exercise their sovereign prerogative. The perfectionists worried that even if the market gave the people what they want, it may not provide them what they *need*.

The perfectionists, of course, grasped the irony of their position—they remained committed to democracy, to the notion that the people should make the ultimate decisions on the merits of substantive public policy, but were not content to leave it to the people to decide what kind of information they should have before making these choices. The perfectionists could be charged with using undemocratic means to preserve democracy, but in truth much of the First Amendment tradition could be faulted on this ground. In protecting the press against state interference, the Supreme Court never assumed that the state was attempting to act in disregard of majority will. On the contrary, the Court knew all too well that state officials were often nothing more than instruments of the majority; yet the Court took upon itself the task of preserving the robustness of public debate and conceived of that ideal just as the perfectionists imagined. *New York Times Co. v. Sullivan* may be ambiguous on this score for, arguably, the Court was frustrating a local majority (Alabama) in favor of a national one. But there is no such ambiguity in the most recent flag-burning case.[8] There the Court used the First Amendment to invalidate a highly popular national statute. It was protecting democracy from itself or, to use another formula, avoiding a tyranny of the majority.

The line between populism and perfectionism was not always clear, and perhaps both strands can be found jumbled in the work of many, myself included, who looked upon the market as a structure of constraint that sometimes sells democratic values short. It is important to emphasize, however, that neither the populists nor the perfectionists wished to replace, destroy, or supplant the market. They fought instead for a series of supplemental, interstitial strategies that when necessary would push the press past the limits of the market, sometimes to the frontier indicated by the phrase "democratically determined speech," sometimes even beyond. They saw the state as an instrument of this policy, and called upon the state to use both its allocative and its regulatory powers for this purpose.

The principal instrument of reform in the allocative sphere was Congress's decision in the mid-1960s, following the recommendation of the Carnegie Commission, to establish and fund the Corporation for Public Broadcasting.[9] This decision was not part of a complicated strategy to undermine the economic autonomy enjoyed by commercial broadcasters, nor a prelude to socializing the press, but rather an effort to introduce into the public square a voice that was not tied to the profit motive. The assumption was that a public broadcasting system would by and large cover issues likely to be slighted by commercial broadcasting but which are nevertheless vital to collective self-governance.

On the regulatory side, the principal corrective for the market was the Fairness Doctrine.[10] This doctrine was created by the Federal Communications Commission (FCC) as an elaboration of its statutory mandate to regulate broadcasters in the public interest. It required broadcasters to cover issues of public importance and to do so in a balanced manner, giving both sides of the story (or as many sides as there might be). As a subsidiary matter, the Fairness Doctrine also gave candidates an opportunity to respond to hostile political editorializing and offered a similar right-of-reply to those who had been personally attacked.

The press fought this regulation as a violation of its freedom, enlisting the support of many academic notables, including, alas, the person I have invoked many times, Harry Kalven, Jr. The issue came to a head in the courts when the author of a book critical of Senator Barry Goldwater appealed to the Supreme Court to uphold his right to respond to a radio broadcast by the Christian Crusade that had accused him of being a Communist sympathizer. The Justices' decision represented a constitutional defeat for the press of some note. In the *Red Lion* decision, one of the last statements of the Warren Court on the First Amendment, the Court came down on the side of the FCC and the Fairness Doctrine.[11] Justice William O. Douglas did not participate, but the other Justices were unanimous. The ruling drew support from all wings of the Court— not just those who are usually identified as the architects of the Warren Court's position on free speech, Hugo Black and William Brennan, but also the conservative Justices John Harlan, Potter Stewart, and Byron White. Indeed, Justice White was the author of the Court's opinion.

White's point was quite simple: The autonomy allowed to the press was not absolute but always reflected an accommodation of competing interests, a synthesis of value and countervalue. In this case the interest offered by the state in support of its regulation—the public's right to be properly informed about issues of public importance—had a particularly compelling quality. Indeed, it made claim to the very same value furthered by the conferral of autonomy: the promotion of a debate on issues of public importance that is "uninhibited, robust, and wide-open."

As use of this talismanic phrase suggests, *Red Lion* was not at war with *New York Times v. Sullivan*. These decisions were in tension in operational detail: *Sullivan* kept the state at bay, while *Red Lion* embraced the state. But *Red Lion* was handed down by the same Court during the same historic period as

Sullivan and rested on *Sullivan*'s animating principle. *Red Lion* and *Sullivan* were seen as companions, as two complementary strategies for furthering the democratic mission of the press and, as such, as part of the same system of free expression.

Sullivan sought to enhance the capacity of the press to report widely and fully on matters of public importance by shielding the press from a form of state action—libel judgments—that might otherwise discourage such reporting. The Fairness Doctrine also sought to broaden the coverage of the press, to make certain that the all-powerful broadcast medium covered issues of public importance and gave listeners or viewers all sides of the story. In upholding that doctrine and the power of the FCC to regulate the press for the purpose of broadening public debate, *Red Lion* affirmed the very same values proclaimed by *Sullivan*.

RED LION was handed down in 1969, a year that marked the beginning of the Nixon presidency and a twenty-five year period of American politics dominated by one theme: the evils of "big government." Republicans controlled the White House for most of this period and called for privatization, deregulation, and balanced budgets. Many of those themes continue to this day, as evidenced by the dramatic expression they were given in the congressional elections of November 1994, but they achieved considerable force during the seventies and eighties, unifying that period and giving it a special character. It is not surprising that in such an environment the nuanced understanding of freedom of the press represented by the fusion of *Red Lion* and *Sullivan* came undone.

The enemies of regulation set their sights on *Red Lion,* and in 1987, after almost two decades of engagement, an amazing victory was achieved. The FCC—not the Supreme Court but the FCC—overturned *Red Lion* and declared the Fairness Doctrine unconstitutional.[12] On review, the Court of Appeals for the District of Columbia upheld the order of the FCC without engaging the constitutional issue, treating it simply as an act of administrative discretion.[13] Congress was of another mind and passed a statute making the Fairness Doctrine a legislative requirement.[14] But President Reagan took the same high ground as the FCC and vetoed the measure on the theory that such regulation is unconstitutional.[15]

Both the FCC and the President pointed to the technological changes—above all, the advent of cable—that have occurred since the days of *Red Lion*. The number of channels available in most homes has mushroomed; now cable subscribers have 50, and soon, we are told, they will have 500.[16] But neither the FCC nor the President addressed the best and most plausible theory of the Fairness Doctrine, which identifies economics, not technology, as the constraining force on the press. The technological revolution now afoot in communications may present us with a large number of channels, but as long as they are all governed by the market, there remains a risk that coverage will be skewed. To embellish on a Bruce Springsteen song, 500 channels and still nothing on.

The FCC's decision contained a line of argument that was commonly employed by those who led the deregulation movement of the 1970s and 1980s: Concede the aspiration but show that the regulation will be counterproductive.[17] Minimum wage laws will not help the poor but rather will make their plight worse by restricting the number of available jobs; employment discrimination laws will not help women but will force them to choose between conforming to the male pattern of full-time employment or dropping out of the market altogether; the Fairness Doctrine will not help produce the rich and varied broadcasting it promises but will rather discourage broadcasters from taking controversial stands. The claim was that the Fairness Doctrine will yield what might more accurately be called "gray speech," not robust public debate. Broadcasters will hesitate to take a strong position on nuclear energy, say, because they know they will have to spend air time presenting the other side or providing opportunities to respond, thereby doubling the economic burden of their public affairs broadcast.

This argument overlooks certain features of the regulatory program—for example, the affirmative obligation to cover issues of public importance—that guarded against the risk of self-censorship. It also overlooks the need for a comparative judgment: even if the regulation produced some measure of self-censorship, broadcasting still might be more varied, more keyed to public issues, if regulated than if not. Admittedly, such a judgment is largely an empirical matter, and while we as citizens might choose to defer to the FCC (if only because it looked at the facts in a systematic way), I believe that Congress had every right to make its own decision on the issue and, furthermore, that the President, who undertook no empirical inquiry whatsoever, had an obligation to defer to it.

In truth, the attack on the Fairness Doctrine was neither technologically nor empirically inspired. It was a battle over ideology and principle, based on conflicting interpretations of the First Amendment and its guarantee of freedom of the press. The FCC and the President believed that the judgment of the Supreme Court in *Red Lion*—specifically that the Fairness Doctrine was consistent with freedom of the press—was simply wrong. Offhand, this might seem to be a gross usurpation by the President and the FCC of a power that rightly belongs to the Supreme Court. After all, we have been taught for almost two centuries now that the Supreme Court is the final arbiter of the Constitution.

In my view, however, the events of 1987 did not constitute

an unconstitutional usurpation. When President Reagan and the FCC repudiated *Red Lion,* they were not taking the law into their own hands but merely drawing the natural and logical conclusions from the doctrine the Supreme Court had developed in the years following that decision. The President and the FCC were only doing what the Supreme Court did not have the opportunity, or perhaps the courage, to do.

This change in constitutional doctrine did not happen all at once but rather at three distinct moments. In the first, *CBS v. DNC,*[18] the Court itself cast doubt upon the constitutional viability of *Red Lion* by drawing a distinction between two questions, permissibility (Is the Fairness Doctrine constitutionally permissible?) and obligation (Is the Fairness Doctrine obligatory?). It then answered the second question in a way that undermined the answer it had given to the first in *Red Lion.*

CBS v. DNC arose in the early 1970s from an attempt by a public interest group to run an "editorial advertisement" on a radio station criticizing the United States' involvement in the Vietnam War. The station refused to run the ad, for purely business reasons, and the FCC refused to require the station to accept the editorial advertisement. In 1973 the Supreme Court—now sharply divided—upheld the decision of the FCC and rested its decision on grounds that ultimately called *Red Lion* into question.

The First Amendment is phrased in negative terms, providing that Congress shall make no law abridging the freedom of the press. Obligations can arise from such negatively worded provisions, but they are remedial in nature and conditioned upon a showing that a state agency violated the provision. A school board has an obligation to desegregate its schools only if it can first be shown to have violated the Equal Protection Clause (also worded negatively) by having operated its schools on a segregated basis. But how, it is fair to ask, could the FCC be deemed to have violated the First Amendment when it seems to have taken no action—when it only refused to order the radio station to revise its policy against accepting editorial advertisements?

Suppose a large number of police officers on duty on a street corner in Manhattan are listening to a soap-box orator denounce the American involvement in Vietnam.[19] An angry crowd approaches the speaker, but the police do nothing. They turn a blind eye, letting the crowd beat and silence the speaker. In this scenario, I think no one would have trouble saying that the police's inaction constituted a form of action and that under the First Amendment the speaker could seek damages against the police or an injunction aimed at preventing future neglect on their part. Inaction does not always equal action, but sometimes it does, in circumstances where we have a right to expect and demand certain action by a state agency. We had such a right in the case of the police, and an analogous one with the FCC. After all, the FCC licenses private institutions to do business, is fully aware of the consequences of its inaction, and is under a statutory duty to make certain that the broadcast industry serves the "public interest."

During the Warren Court era, inaction was ordinarily treated as action when a special relationship, such as that between licensee and licensor, existed.[20] In 1973, when *CBS v. DNC* was handed down, those precedents still had considerable force, as the transition from one judicial era to the next had not yet been fully effectuated. Thus, the Supreme Court's decision to uphold the FCC could not be seen as resting on the view that the FCC had not "acted" in the constitutionally relevant sense. It is far more plausible to read the Court's decision as resting on other grounds, and in that vein two propositions suggest themselves: (1) the radio station, but not the crowd in my example, could make claim to the First Amendment to protect its behavior, or (2) the refusal of the radio station to carry editorial advertisements posed less of a threat to First Amendment values than did the crowd beating a street-corner speaker.

The first of these propositions denies that the jurisdiction of the state to regulate the press is as great as its authority to regulate the behavior of a crowd. The second doubts whether the goal to be served by state regulation of the radio station is compelling. Although either proposition makes the FCC's decision not to intervene more justifiable than the analogous decision of the police in the hypothetical case of the street-corner speaker, it should be emphasized that relying on either or both of these propositions tended to undermine *Red Lion*. They rendered suspect any effort by the FCC to regulate the radio station in order to broaden its reportage.

In *CBS v. DNC* the Court distinguished the permissibility question from the obligation question. Soon thereafter the Court introduced another distinction into the law—this time between broadcasting and publishing—and cast further doubt on the validity of *Red Lion*. In the new case, *Miami Herald v. Tornillo*,[21] the Court invalidated a Florida right-to-reply statute even though that law operated in much the same manner as the Fairness Doctrine. In the *Miami Herald* case, a union official running for the Florida legislature wanted to respond to a vicious editorial in the city's leading newspaper and was authorized to do so by the state statute. The Court's decision rebuffing the official and striking down the statute was presented as necessary to protect the autonomy of editors to decide what to publish and how. But once it became law, there was reason to ask, as the FCC and the President eventually did (though only rhetorically): Why aren't broadcasters entitled to the same measure of autonomy as newspapers? After all, they are also part of the press.

One possible answer emphasizes the difference in the source of the property rights of the various media. The property rights of a newspaper are shaped by many forces, including the common law and statutes that are, by and large, applicable to all businesses. Broadcasters operate under these same laws but have one additional property right—an exclusive license giving them permission to use a particular broadcast frequency. This license is conferred by a deliberate and institutionally specific decision by the state intended to avoid interferences on the electromagnetic spectrum.

Admittedly, this licensing arrangement is relevant in a case like *CBS v. DNC* for deciding whether the failure of the FCC to regulate broadcasters in a certain way is a form of action. In such a case, the Court is deciding whether the FCC has an *obligation* to regulate. But the presence of the licensing connection has no relevance when the question before the Court is whether it is *permissible* for the state to regulate. The state can regulate a wholly private entity, licensed or unlicensed. In addressing the permissibility question, the Court is determining the scope of the autonomy conferred by the First Amendment, which, in turn, should depend on the function of the institution in society and what it needs to perform that role, not on the source of its property rights or the particular dynamics that gave rise to them. In setting the bounds of autonomy allowed by the rule of *New York Times Co. v. Sullivan*, the Court has always looked to social function, not the source of property rights, and in that context has held broadcasting and newspapers to the exact same standard.

In rejecting this approach and thus drawing a distinction between publishing and broadcasting, the Court encircled *Red Lion* and narrowed its scope, just as it had done the year before. In *CBS v. DNC* the Court held that although it was constitutionally permissible for the FCC to regulate broadcasters in order to protect the robustness of public debate, there was no obligation on the FCC to further that value. Now, as *Miami*

Herald proclaimed, the state was prohibited from regulating newspapers to achieve the same end. Moreover, like *CBS v. DNC*, *Miami Herald* rested on premises that cast serious doubt upon the continued validity of even so narrow a ruling. The Court spoke of the Florida statute as though it were imposing a "penalty" on the newspaper for expressing its view,[22] a wholly unjustified characterization but a characterization which, if it could be applied to the Florida right-of-reply statute, could be applied to the Fairness Doctrine (and, for that matter, to any kind of libel action, even the type allowed under *New York Times Co. v. Sullivan*). To resolve the conflict with *Red Lion*, *Miami Herald* employed a technique that a literary critic might call erasure by omission: it did not cite, refer to, distinguish, or in any way even mention *Red Lion*. Perhaps the author of the Court's opinion in *Miami Herald*, Chief Justice Warren Burger, thought *Red Lion* would simply go away if he pretended that it did not exist.

CBS v. DNC was decided in 1973, *Miami Herald* in 1974. For the remainder of the decade, *Red Lion* seemed a precedent of little force. Then, in 1981, the Court upheld a special provision of the Communications Act that prohibited willful and repeated refusals by broadcasters to sell air time to legally qualified candidates for federal office.[23] This decision gave some life to *Red Lion*—here it was actually cited—but only to a limited degree. Most thought the 1981 decision reflected a special accommodation to the federal electoral process and a determined effort by Congress to reform it.

In 1986, as the privatization and deregulation movement gained greater and greater strength and the more extravagant versions of capitalism and liberalism seized the zeitgeist, the Court found in the interstices of the First Amendment a right that made *Red Lion* and all that it stood for even more untenable: the right not to have unwelcome words put in one's mouth. Despite its unexpected source, the announcement of this right constituted the third, and perhaps most decisive, blow to *Red Lion*.

In the case in question, *Pacific Gas & Electric Co. v. Public Utilities Commission*,[24] the California utility commission required a power company to allow a citizen group that monitored the rate-setting process to use the so-called extra space in the utility company's billing envelope to reach the public. The "extra space" was the room in the envelope that could accommodate an insert without increasing the minimum postage charge. That space had been used in the past by the power company for distributing its own newsletter, "Progress," and was now allocated by the utility commission to the citizen group four times a year. The rationale for the regulation was the same as that underlying the Fairness Doctrine or the Florida right-to-reply statute—to give the public both sides of the story. In striking down the regulation, the Court did not dispute the need for the citizen group's information, nor did it doubt the worthiness of the purpose of the regulation, but thought the First Amendment, as a matter of principle, prohibited the state from requiring the power company to carry in its billing envelope a message that the company found offensive or odious or with which it disagreed.

Although the context seems highly specialized, the significance of *Pacific Gas & Electric* for state regulation of the press was immediately recognized. The author of the plurality opinion, Justice Lewis Powell, made reference to the earlier decision of the Court invalidating the Florida right-to-reply statute to support his decision,[25] and when, the very next year, the FCC took on the Fairness Doctrine and announced it would no longer follow *Red Lion*, it relied in part on *Pacific Gas & Electric*.[26] If it violates the First Amendment to require a utility company to carry in its billing envelope a message that it finds offensive, it should be equally unlawful, so the FCC reasoned, to require a network to broadcast a show that it finds objectionable.

Regulations of the type involved in *Red Lion* or *Pacific Gas & Electric* entailed a compromise of the company's property rights and a loss of the economic value associated with those rights. The mandated message or program necessarily displaced an article or program that a company deemed more profitable. The company's displaced message can only be carried if extra pages are added or the broadcast day extended or, in the case of the power company, extra postage is added. Although the economic loss may be small, its reality cannot be denied.

This economic loss is of no constitutional significance, however, certainly not under the First Amendment, and not even under the provision of the Fifth Amendment which mandates that no property shall be taken for public use without compensation. The economic loss is neither severe nor localized, and thus, in contrast to a state's decision to condemn a private home in order to erect a highway, presents none of the special conditions that are required to transform a regulation into a taking or confiscation of property.

In fact, the Justices appeared unanimous in *Pacific Gas & Electric* in denying that the regulation by the utility commission amounted to a confiscation of the power company's property; and in reaching that conclusion they gave no weight to the fact that the power company was a regulated monopoly. A few years earlier the Court rejected an analogous claim for compensation and upheld a decision of the California Supreme Court that gave political activists, as a matter of state law, access to a private shopping center.[27] The same principle controlled in *Pacific Gas & Electric* and presumably would apply to the press.

The free speech claim upheld in *Pacific Gas & Electric* arose not from the economic loss suffered but rather from the fact that the owners of the company were being compelled to support financially views or ideas to which they did not subscribe and in fact actually detested. It is hard, however, to turn this objection into a viable principle of constitutional law without dismantling the modern democratic state. The entire taxation system is predicated on the notion that money taken from citizens may be used to support activities that some or many detest: wars, the construction of ugly highways and office buildings, parades, lectures at state universities, and many of the books on the shelves of the public libraries. Such compelled financial support is seen as an obligation of citizenship, necessary to serve community purposes. With regulations of the type we are considering—those that give political activists reasonable access to the public—the community purpose is the preservation of the democratic process itself. Having one's property or wealth used to support activities that one detests is widely held to be a price of citizenship in a democracy.

When the power of the state is exercised not through taxation but through a grant of access to someone's property or through a requirement that a station present an argument or viewpoint it does not believe, there is an additional risk. The views expressed may be attributed by the audience to the publisher or station or, in the case of *Pacific Gas & Electric,* to the power company, rather than to the person or organization given access. That is why the right evoked in *Pacific Gas & Electric* is variously described not as a right not to speak but as a right against forced association or, even better, a right against false attribution. It is doubtful, however, that anyone would falsely attribute the ideas presented in the citizen group's newsletter to the utility company or, in the press context, to the publisher or the television station. In any event, the danger of false attribution can be dealt with by a disclaimer that, for example, "the ideas presented are not those of the station"; a blanket denial of regulatory power is not necessary.

IN 1987 the FCC decided that the Fairness Doctrine was unconstitutional, and President Reagan took a similar position in vetoing the congressional effort to restore it. In these actions, as we have seen, the FCC and the President were not taking the law into their own hands but only drawing the obvious conclusion from the three decisions—*CBS v. DNC, Miami Herald,* and *Pacific Gas & Electric*—that emptied *Red Lion* of its animating spirit and put an end to the effort to limit the autonomy of the press in the name of freedom.

In the years immediately following the confrontation of 1987, Congress has been unable to reinstate the Fairness Doctrine, and the political forces that might have be expected to look upon it with favor seem to have turned elsewhere. Even Mario Cuomo has chosen to denounce it.[28] In 1992, however, Congress enacted a measure that regulated the cable industry in the name of these same values, and in June 1994 the Supreme Court handed down a decision, *Turner Broadcasting System v. FCC,*[29] that spoke to the constitutionality of that regulation. The Court's decision revealed how empty a precedent *Red Lion* had finally become.

The statute challenged in *Turner Broadcasting* did not regulate a familiar member of the press—a newspaper or a television or radio station—but rather cable operators. Cable operators are the gatekeepers of the cable industry. They purchase programs from outside sources, including broadcasters and cable programmers, and then transmit these programs to subscribers in much the way that the telephone company transmits voices. A wire brings the signal of the cable operator into the house.

Cable operators need to use public streets and rights of way for their wires, and accordingly they are licensed or franchised by a city or state government. Most localities are served by only one cable operator. In the 1992 Cable Act, Congress sought to regulate the power of cable operators to choose among its sources of programming; it required that a certain number of cable channels be committed to retransmitting the programs of local broadcasters.[30] This would limit the channels available for cable programmers, and they joined the cable operators in their effort to overturn the Act.

Over the years the cable industry has grown enormously. Today, sixty percent of American homes with television sets subscribe to cable. That still leaves forty percent dependent on broadcasting for their television, however. In some instances, cable is not available in the area; in others, persons cannot afford the fee to subscribe or choose to put their money elsewhere. Congress feared that cable operators, who are sometimes economically tied to cable programmers, might decide not to carry or retransmit the programs of local broadcasters. This action by cable operators would impair the economic position of the broadcasting industry, perhaps bringing it to the point of collapse. Once broadcasters failed, many homes—some portion of the forty percent that do not now have cable—would not be served by any television whatsoever. The must-carry provisions of the 1992 regulation could be seen as a protection against this risk's ever materializing.

In the days of *Red Lion, Turner Broadcasting* would have been an easy case, but twenty-five years later all the premises had changed. The Court was fragmented, and no majority could be found to uphold the congressional regulation. All that unified the Court was a distrust of government. One block of Justices, which included Ruth Bader Ginsburg and Sandra Day O'Connor, as well as Antonin Scalia and Clarence Thomas, took this distrust to an extreme. They declared the must-carry provisions of the 1992 Cable Act a violation of the First Amendment.

Another group of four manifested their distrust by remanding the case for yet another round of litigation. The trial court was instructed to scrutinize more rigorously the stated purpose of Congress and the means chosen to further those ends. Is the broadcasting industry genuinely in jeopardy? Might there be less restrictive means for achieving this purpose? On both these issues, the burden of proof was squarely placed on the shoulders of the government, not on those attacking the regulation (cable operators and programmers). Also, a certain willingness to second-guess Congress was manifest. Justice Anthony Kennedy, principal spokesperson for this group, reminded the trial court to which the case was remanded of the obligation of the judiciary "to exercise independent judgment when First Amendment rights are implicated."[31] Overlooking the fact that the First Amendment was on both sides of the issue—it informed the interest served by the congressional legislation as well as the one threatened by it—Kennedy insisted that it was the job of the judiciary "to assure that, in formulating its judgments, Congress has drawn reasonable inferences based on substantial evidence."[32]

The ninth Justice—John Paul Stevens—was prepared to uphold the 1992 Act. He did not dispute Justice Kennedy's formulation of the standard of review; in declaring the 1992 Act lawful, he simply applied that standard differently to the existing record and came to the opposite conclusion. In the end, however, he backed away from this conclusion and supported the position Kennedy had taken: remand for another trial. Justice Stevens justified this odd reversal as needed to form a judgment for the Court. His willingness to compromise might be taken as a fair indication of either his sense of institutional responsibility or the shallowness of his attachment to the views he expressed, or both.

Large portions of Justice Kennedy's opinion did not focus on the immediate issue before the Court—the constitutionality of the must-carry provisions of the 1992 Cable Act—but instead provided a primer on the cable industry and on the constitutional principles governing the press. (Before becoming a Justice, Anthony Kennedy had been a law professor in California.) These portions of his opinion—*obiter dictum*, if I ever saw it—were endorsed by a majority of the Justices; in fact, his description of the cable industry was "unanimous." In this exposition *Red Lion* made an appearance and was treated as though it were good law, without mention of the constitutional confrontation of 1987. This was, however, simply a judicial courtesy.

For one thing, Kennedy mentioned *Red Lion* only to limit it strictly to broadcasting. According to Kennedy, "The justification for our distinct approach to broadcast regulation rests upon the unique physical limitations of the broadcast medium."[33] He was referring to the fact that broadcasters transmit their signal in unique bands on the electromagnetic spectrum and that noninterfering frequencies are, as a purely physical matter, scarce or limited. Kennedy acknowledged that "courts and commentators have criticized the scarcity rationale since its inception,"[34] but he refused to transcend the bounds that rationale placed on *Red Lion*. Indeed, he refused to extend the *Red Lion* approach to cable operators even though he repeatedly spoke of them as exercising "bottleneck monopoly power."[35] Under these circumstances, it is hard to think of *Red Lion* and its endorsement of state power as anything other than a stray, living at the margins of the law, a formal vestige of another era, soon to be overtaken by technological advances that will shrink almost to nothing the practical significance of the domain it controls.

On the other hand, the branch of constitutional law that endows the press with an almost absolute autonomy from access regulations of the type endorsed in *Red Lion—Miami Herald* and *Pacific Gas & Electric*—is treated in Kennedy's opinion as being in full force. According to him, the must-carry provisions of the 1992 Cable Act should be governed by an intermediate, as opposed to strict, standard of review, but only because he is able to distinguish them from *Miami Herald* and *Pacific Gas & Electric*. The laws in those cases, he insisted, were content regulations, requiring the strictest scrutiny. He was unwilling to characterize the must-carry provisions of the 1992 Act in similar terms and thus was able to judge them under the laxer standard. Kennedy argued that the protection for broadcasting was not content based, but rather was predicated on a desire to ensure a continuation of television service to the forty percent of American homes without cable.

The four dissenters bitterly complained of this feature of Kennedy's analysis. They saw the must-carry provision as a species of content regulation pure and simple and thus subject to the most exacting scrutiny—a scrutiny that few laws can survive. They claimed that must-carry provisions privileging local broadcasters over potential cable programmers necessarily entailed a preference for the content of broadcast television. The dissenters considered the possible justifications for such a preference—a "diversity of viewpoints," "localism," or "education," in Justice O'Connor's terms—but not surprisingly found them all wanting under the rigors of strict scrutiny. This test requires that the end served by a law be compelling and that the means employed in the law be almost perfectly adapted for the pursuit of that end.

Since the dissenters were prepared to strike down the must-carry provisions of the 1992 Cable Act on these grounds, it is not difficult to imagine what they would do with a law that sought to regulate the press in the mode the FCC once did in

Red Lion. Such a law is clearly an instance of content regulation, and if the desire to present the public with a diversity of viewpoints is not sufficient to justify the must-carry provisions of the 1992 Cable Act, it is hard to see how it could justify the Fairness Doctrine. Justice O'Connor was one vote short of a majority in *Turner Broadcasting* itself, but on this larger issue she seemed to capture the spirit of the entire Court. Because Kennedy applied a laxer standard of review, he did not need to address the questions O'Connor did, specifically whether diversity of viewpoints, localism, or education were compelling interests. But that seemed to be Kennedy's essential strategy—at all costs, avoid the characterization that the must-carry provisions are a species of content regulation, even to the point of denying that public broadcasting, also preferred by the must-carry provisions, tends to be educational or otherwise have any special content. His efforts to implement this strategy appear so studied and so strained as to suggest that if the must-carry provisions were a form of content regulation—for example, intended to present the public with a diversity of viewpoints or otherwise enhance public understanding—he or someone else who joined him would have sided with O'Connor and voted to strike down the law. In the end, a majority of the Justices were persuaded to remand the 1992 Cable Act for further factual inquiries, placing all the burdens on the government, but it is unlikely that they would be so indecisive with a law that specifically limited the autonomy of the press in order to assure full and ample coverage of matters of public importance. Content regulation is content regulation, even if the entity being regulated operates under a government license—as a reference to *Pacific Gas & Electric* makes clear.

In the domain of allocations, state programs seeking to diversify the press have fared much better, at least at the constitutional level. In 1990 a closely divided Supreme Court upheld the congressionally mandated policy of the FCC that gave preference to racial minorities in the award or assignment of broadcasting licenses. The assumption in that case, *Metro Broadcasting, Inc. v. FCC*,[36] was that race is a proxy for viewpoint and that minority owners would exercise the discretion allowed to them by the market—however small that might be—to diversify programming and thus to enrich public debate.

The Justices divided over the equal protection claim. Justice Brennan used Justice Powell's opinion in *Bakke*[37] as his guide and formed a majority to uphold the FCC. He ruled that the FCC's desire to obtain a diversity of viewpoints was a sufficiently worthy purpose to justify the use of race in the allocative process. If diversity can justify affirmative action in higher education, it should be sufficient to justify it on the air waves. Once again, the dissenting position was primarily articulated by Justice O'Connor. She objected to the laxness of the standard of review used by Justice Brennan—in her view, only compelling purposes could justify racial preferences, and diversity of viewpoints lacked that urgent quality. She also thought using race as an allocative criterion was an inadequate means of assuring that diversity; race is not tied to viewpoint. Justice Brennan countered by pointing to the role Congress played in the formation of that policy and explained why it is good and proper for the Court to show that institution a measure of deference. In the end, Brennan had his way in *Metro Broadcasting*, but the balance of power soon shifted. On the very day that decision was handed down, Brennan retired from the Court, and a number of others who formed his majority soon followed—first Marshall (1991), then White (1993), and then Blackmun (1994). By June 1995 O'Connor was able to form a new majority dedicated to overruling *Metro Broadcasting* on the racial issue.[38] All racial preferences must be judged by the strictest of scrutiny.

On the matter of free speech, however, *Metro Broadcasting*

can be read as a more durable but somewhat unusual precedent—law by assumption. Its power in this domain derived
from the fact that no one voiced a First Amendment objection
to the policy of the FCC. O'Connor expressed some qualms
with measures "designed to amplify a distinct set of views or
the views of a particular class of speakers,"[39] but for the most
part all the Justices assumed that the First Amendment did not
prevent the FCC from allocating broadcast licenses in such a
way as to create program diversity or otherwise enhance the
robustness of public debate. In this respect, the FCC was the
beneficiary of the constitutional indifference to allocations that
surfaced so clearly in *Rust v. Sullivan*. In *Rust* the Court upheld
a regulation that prohibited employees of federally funded family planning clinics from advocating on behalf of the right to
undergo an abortion, though they were free to advocate
against it. This ruling manifested a constitutional indifference
to the way the government manages its allocative programs,
and though that indifference is problematic as a purely theoretical matter, it has certain practical benefits: Content judgments are allowed the state. The Court's stance on allocations
saved the preferential policies at issue in *Metro Broadcasting*
from a First Amendment attack and might even help keep
public broadcasting alive.

Over the years political opposition to the use of federal funds
to support public broadcasting has been growing, and in the
months following the congressional elections of November
1994 this opposition has been especially fierce. This has occurred against a background which assumes—incorrectly, I
believe—that the Constitution is indifferent as to the existence
of public broadcasting. This indifference has aided the opposition in the limited sense that it has remitted the defenders of
public broadcasting to the fortunes of politics; but so far not
one opponent has contended that the Corporation for Public

Broadcasting is unconstitutional. We should be grateful for that, but I cannot help wondering whether it is only a matter of time before *Pacific Gas & Electric,* one of the principal instruments used by the present Court to curb the regulatory state, will be used to create a constitutional doubt about the allocative state and its programs to broaden the coverage of the press.

Some read *Pacific Gas & Electric* as resting on the rule against content regulation. A far more plausible interpretation sees it as affirming the right of citizens not to have their property used by the government to support an activity they detest. The affirmation of this right occurred in the regulatory context, but it seems fair to ask whether that right might also bar the government from using any taxes collected from citizens to support programs or publications that present views they find abhorrent. In *Pacific Gas & Electric* itself, Justice Powell's opinion contained a single sentence disclaiming any intent to limit the state's power to allocate; he thought the regulation of the utility commission unconstitutional but said he saw no objection to having the commission subsidize the public interest group's activities out of funds generated through a tax on the utility. Yet I wonder whether, in time, the logic of the decision will overwhelm his disclaimer.

In the spring of 1993 Judge Morris Arnold of the Eighth Circuit—appointed to the federal district court by President Reagan and then elevated to the Court of Appeals by President Bush, and a favorite on the lecture circuit of the Federalist Society—delivered a lecture at the Yale Law School arguing for an extension of the principle of *Pacific Gas & Electric* to the allocative domain. He chose his target well: the NEA, which, in the wake of the Mapplethorpe controversy, stands as the most vulnerable of all speech-related subsidy programs. Some liberals are as doubtful about its constitutionality as are the conservatives. But if *Pacific Gas & Electric* can be applied to the NEA and be used to render that allocative program unconstitutional, certainly a similar argument can be voiced against the Corporation for Public Broadcasting. In that instance, the allocative state will, as a matter of constitutional law, have been brought under the same regime that now governs the regulatory one; free press will have become reduced to free enterprise, and the fate of our democracy will be placed wholly in the hands of the market.

THE CHALLENGE AHEAD

4

The law never changes all at once—new law builds on the old. But at some point the changes become so numerous and so firmly entrenched that we can declare a new beginning. Over the past twenty-five years a new Court has come into being, and with it a new First Amendment jurisprudence.

This new jurisprudence is defined by a number of decisions that have figured prominently in current debates: on issues relating to the press, *Miami Herald* and *Pacific Gas & Electric;* on campaign finance, *Buckley v. Valeo;* on hate speech and arguably the feminist campaign against pornography, *R.A.V. v. St. Paul;* and on public funding of speech-related activities, including the arts, *Rust v. Sullivan.* These five decisions represent a turn away from a democratic theory of the First Amendment and a move toward a more libertarian one. Common to all these decisions is a marked hostility toward the state and a refusal to acknowledge the role the state can play in furthering freedom of speech.

In the allocative context, this outlook resulted in a conception of speech-related subsidies as nothing more than gifts, which has led to a willingness—so manifest in *Rust v. Sullivan*—to tolerate virtually any limits on subsidy programs, even those that distort public discourse. The Court has refused to acknowledge the possibility that subsidies might well serve First Amendment purposes by freeing education, libraries, art, and other activities that enrich public deliberations from a strict dependence on the market and aggregations of private wealth.

In the regulatory sphere, this same wariness toward the state has had even more unfortunate consequences: It yielded not just an indifference to but rather an invalidation of a wide variety of legislative and executive measures intended to grant citizens more equality in the public arena and to promote free and open debate. Struck down were a congressional enactment that limited campaign expenditures (in *Buckley v. Valeo*); a municipal ordinance regulating hate speech (in *R.A.V. v. St. Paul*); a state statute granting access to newspapers for the purpose of replying to personal attacks (in *Miami Herald*); and a regulation of a state utility commission that conferred access to a citizens' group (in *Pacific Gas & Electric*). The force of these decisions were manifest in the *Turner Broadcasting* debacle of 1994, which left the 1992 Cable Act still in doubt. They were even more in play in the odd constitutional confrontation of 1987, when the FCC refused to follow *Red Lion* and President Reagan declared Congress's effort to restore the Fairness Doctrine unconstitutional and vetoed it.

The new jurisprudence reflected the popular political philosophy of its time. The 1970s and 1980s in America were characterized by calls for deregulation, rhetoric about balanced budgets, taxpayer revolts, the New Federalism, and privatization. The tenets of orthodox capitalism and classical liberalism achieved great currency, and they received dramatic and only slightly belated confirmation by developments in the East: the revolutions in Eastern Europe in 1989 and the eventual collapse of the Soviet Union in 1991. Save for the Carter intermezzo (1976 to 1980), in which no vacancies occurred on the High Court, the Republicans controlled the White House for a quarter century and during this period made decisive appointments to the Court. By 1992, when George Bush was defeated and Bill Clinton elected, Republicans had appointed eight of the nine sitting Justices. Byron White was the only Justice who remained from the days of the Warren Court.

These fortuities of history no doubt account for many of the changes in Supreme Court doctrine and for the emergence of a new outlook on the First Amendment. But too heavy an emphasis on these historical developments and the resulting personnel changes might mislead in one important respect: It risks trivializing the shift in doctrine and creates the mistaken impression that delivery from the new First Amendment jurisprudence is easily at hand—that a few more appointments are all that is needed. In my view something much deeper is afoot. Granted, a number of the crucial decisions of the Burger and Rehnquist Courts sharply divided the Justices, and it is therefore quite conceivable, maybe even likely, that with a different group of Justices a different result would have been reached. *Buckley v. Valeo, Rust v. Sullivan,* and *R.A.V. v. St. Paul* might fit this description. But this most certainly is not the case with *Miami Herald* and *Pacific Gas & Electric,* crucial precedents for the *Turner Broadcasting* decision, and even more tellingly in the Court's 1995 decision involving the Boston St. Patrick's Day parade. In the Boston case Justice Souter wrote an opinion that all other Justices, including the two Clinton appointees, joined. Souter held unconstitutional a requirement that an Irish-American gay, lesbian, and bisexual group be allowed to participate in the parade.[1] That requirement, Souter reasoned, violated the principles of *Miami Herald* and *Pacific Gas &*

Electric that gave the speaker the "autonomy to choose the content of his own message."[2]

Miami Herald was virtually a unanimous decision, and though *Pacific Gas & Electric* divided the Court, both Justice Marshall and Justice Brennan—architects of much of the jurisprudence of the Warren Court—were part of the majority. There was a separate concurrence by Brennan in *Miami Herald* and one by Marshall in *Pacific Gas & Electric*, sure signs of their unease, but in the end they cast their lot with the majority. It is possible that these two giants of the law had a temporary lapse or were themselves captured by the times, but it is equally possible that they saw in the resurgent libertarianism of *Miami Herald* and *Pacific Gas & Electric* a truth from which they could not shake themselves.

The appeal of a decision like *Miami Herald* is easy to understand. Although it curbed the power of the state to broaden public discussion, it accords well with the tradition of autonomy long enjoyed by the press in this country. The arguments of *Pacific Gas & Electric* may seem more contrived—no more than a clever transmogrification of a failed property claim into speech—but that reading ignores the roots of that decision in the First Amendment tradition. In striking down the California regulation, Justice Powell made an appeal to one of the most venerable precedents of American constitutional law—the 1943 decision in *West Virginia v. Barnette*.[3] In this heroic decision the Supreme Court resisted the patriotic fervor sweeping the nation and chose rather to protect the right of Jehovah's Witness schoolchildren to refuse to salute the flag, in keeping with their religious principles.

I appreciate the appeal of *Barnette* for the Court, and for Marshall and Brennan in particular, but it also seems to me that a crucial distinction was lost. In *Barnette* the power of the state was being used to perpetuate an orthodoxy or to impose a dogma, and thus rightly should be curbed. By contrast, in *Pacific Gas & Electric, Miami Herald,* and the other cases that bespeak of the First Amendment libertarianism, the state had another purpose in mind. The state, through regulation, was trying to enhance the robustness of public debate, not impose an orthodoxy, and had chosen a means seemingly well fitted to serve that end. In this context, the rule of *Barnette,* so noble in its conception, seems entirely misplaced. The autonomy protected by the First Amendment and rightly enjoyed by individuals and the press is not an end in itself, as it might be in some moral code, but is rather a means to further the democratic values underlying the Bill of Rights.

What is needed, therefore, is not a few more appointments (though they will help) but an improved sense of proportion. We must learn to embrace a truth that is full of irony and contradiction: that the state can be both an enemy and a friend of speech; that it can do terrible things to undermine democracy but some wonderful things to enhance it as well. This, I fear, is a complicated truth, far more complicated than we have allowed ourselves to admit for some time now, but which is still—I hope—not beyond our reach.

NOTES

—

INTRODUCTION

1. See Alexander Meiklejohn, *Political Freedom: The Constitutional Powers of the People* (New York: Harper, 1960; repr. Westport, Conn.: Greenwood Press, 1979); "The First Amendment Is an Absolute," *Supreme Court Review* (1961):245–266. See also Harry Kalven, Jr., "The New York Times Case: A Note on 'The Central Meaning of the First Amendment,'" *Supreme Court Review* (1964):191–222.

2. Robert H. Bork, "Neutral Principles and Some First Amendment Problems," *Indiana Law Journal* 47 (1971):1–35.

3. William J. Brennan, Jr., "The Supreme Court and the Meiklejohn Interpretation of the First Amendment," *Harvard Law Review* 79 (1965):1–20; see also Justice Brennan's remarks in "Address," *Rutgers Law Review* 32 (1979):173–183. For a consideration of the various theories of the First Amendment, see Lee C. Bollinger, "Free Speech and Intellectual Values," *Yale Law Journal* 92 (1983):438–473; Owen M. Fiss, "Why the State?" in *Liberalism Divided* (Boulder: Westview, 1996); Paul G. Stern, "A Pluralistic Reading of the First Amendment and Its Relation to Public Discourse," *Yale Law Journal* 99 (1990):925–944.

4. New York Times Co. v. Sullivan, 376 U.S. 254, 270 (1964).

I. THE SILENCING EFFECT OF SPEECH

1. Harry Kalven, Jr., *A Worthy Tradition: Freedom of Speech in America*, ed. Jamie Kalven (New York: Harper & Row, 1988), p. xxii.

2. Ibid.

3. See Harry Kalven, Jr., *The Negro and the First Amendment* (Chicago: University of Chicago Press, 1966).

4. 388 U.S. 307 (1967). See also Justice Black's dissent in Brown v. Louisiana, 383 U.S. 131, 151 (1966).

5. 376 U.S. 254 (1964).

6. 395 U.S. 444 (1969).

7. New York Times Co. v. United States, 403 U.S. 713 (1971).

8. Harry Kalven, Jr., "Even When a Nation Is at War," *Harvard Law Review* 85 (1971):3–36, pp. 25–36. See also Owen M. Fiss, "Free Speech and the Prior Restraint Doctrine," in *Liberalism Divided* (Boulder: Westview, 1996).

9. 347 U.S. 483 (1954).

10. 410 U.S. 113 (1973).

11. See Planned Parenthood v. Casey, 505 U.S. 833 (1992); see also Ruth Bader Ginsburg, "Speaking in a Judicial Voice," *New York University Law Review* 67 (1992):1185–1209, pp. 1199–1201; Guido Calabresi, "Antidiscrimination and Constitutional Accountability (What the Bork-Brennan Debate Ignores)," *Harvard Law Review* 105 (1991):80–151; Owen M. Fiss, "What Is Feminism?" *Arizona State Law Journal* 26 (1994):413–428.

12. *Civil Rights Act of 1964*, Pub. L. No. 88-352, 78 Stat. 241 (1964); *Voting Rights Act of 1965*, Pub. L. No. 89-110, 79 Stat. 437 (1965); *Civil Rights Act of 1968*, Pub. L. No. 90-284, 82 Stat. 73 (1968).

13. See William N. Eskridge, Jr., "Reneging on History? Playing the Court/Congress/President Civil Rights Game," *California Law Review* 79 (1991):613–684.

14. *Voting Rights Act Amendments of 1982*, Pub. L. No. 97-205, 96 Stat. 131 (1982); *Americans with Disabilities Act of 1990*, Pub. L. No. 101-336, 104 Stat. 327 (1990); *Civil Rights Act of 1991*, Pub. L. No. 102-166, 105 Stat. 1071 (1991).

15. See Frank I. Michelman, "On Protecting the Poor Through the Fourteenth Amendment," *Harvard Law Review* 83 (1969):7–59; "In Pursuit of Constitutional Welfare Rights: One View of Rawls' Theory of Justice," *University of Pennsylvania Law Review* 121 (1973):962–1019; "Welfare Rights in a Constitutional Democracy," *Washington University Law Quarterly* (1979):659–685.

16. United States v. Eichman, 496 U.S. 310 (1990); Texas v. Johnson, 491 U.S. 397 (1989). See *Measures to Protect the American Flag: Hearings before the Senate Comm. on the Judiciary Proposing an Amendment to the Constitution Authorizing the Congress and the States to Prohibit the Physical Desecration of the American Flag*, 101st. Cong., 2d

Sess. (1990); *Measures to Protect the Physical Integrity of the American Flag: Hearings before the Senate Comm. on the Judiciary*, 101st Cong., 1st Sess. (1989); *Statutory and Constitutional Responses to the Supreme Court Decision in Texas v. Johnson: Hearings before the Subcomm. on Civil and Constitutional Rights of the House Comm. on the Judiciary*, 101st Cong., 1st Sess. (1989); Frank I. Michelman, "Saving Old Glory: On Constitutional Iconography," *Stanford Law Review* 42 (1990):1337–1364; Sheldon H. Nahmod, "The Sacred Flag and the First Amendment," *Indiana Law Journal* 66 (1991):511–548. The issue has not gone away, and the debate is now centering around a constitutional amendment. See Steve Goldstein, "Flag Debate Stirs Red, White, Blue Passions," *New York Times*, July 3, 1995, A1, col. 1. The effort to adopt an amendment that overrides the Supreme Court recently failed in the Senate, but only by three votes. Robin Toner, "Flag-Burning Amendment Fails in Senate, but Margin Narrows," *New York Times*, December 13, 1995, A1, col. 1.

17. See Mari J. Matsuda, Charles R. Lawrence III, Richard Delgado, and Kimberlè Williams Crenshaw, *Words That Wound: Critical Race Theory, Assaultive Speech, and the First Amendment* (Boulder: Westview Press, 1993).

18. See Catharine A. MacKinnon, *Only Words* (Cambridge: Harvard University Press, 1993); *Feminism Unmodified: Discourses on Life and Law* (Cambridge: Harvard University Press, 1987), pp. 127–213; *Toward a Feminist Theory of the State* (Cambridge: Harvard University Press, 1989). See also Andrea Dworkin and Catharine A. MacKinnon, *Pornography and Civil Rights: A New Day for Women's Equality* (Minneapolis: Organizing Against Pornography, 1988).

19. See Kenneth J. Levit, "Campaign Finance Reform and the Return of Buckley v. Valeo," *Yale Law Journal* 103 (1993):469–503. See also Lillian R. BeVier, "Money and Politics: A Perspective on the First Amendment and Campaign Finance Reform," *California Law Review* 73 (1985):1045–1090; Vincent Blasi, "Free Speech and the Widening Gyre of Fund-Raising: Why Campaign Spending Limits May Not Violate the First Amendment After All," *Columbia Law Review* 94 (1994):1281–1325.

20. See Owen M. Fiss, "The Fate of an Idea Whose Time Has Come: Antidiscrimination Law in the Second Decade after *Brown v. Board of Education*," *University of Chicago Law Review* 41 (1974):742–773. See also *The Civil Rights Act of 1964: Text, Analysis, Legislative History—What It Means to Employers, Businessmen, Unions, Employees, Minority Groups* (Washington, D.C.: Bureau of National Affairs, 1964).

21. This formulation was used by Edmond Cahn during the McCarthy

88

period. Edmond Cahn, "The Firstness of the First Amendment," *Yale Law Journal* 65 (1956):464–481. Another formulation can be found in Robert B. McKay, "The Preference for Freedom," *New York University Law Review* 34 (1959):1182–1227.

22. MacKinnon, *Only Words*, pp. 29–41. See generally Ronald Dworkin, "Women and Pornography," *New York Review of Books*, October 21, 1993, vol. 40, p. 36, n. 17.

23. Thomas I. Emerson, *The System of Freedom of Expression* (New York: Random House, 1970); "Pornography and the First Amendment: A Reply to Professor MacKinnon," *Yale Law and Policy Review* 3 (1984):130–143.

24. See New York Times Co. v. United States, 403 U.S. 713, 714–720 (1971) (Black, J., concurring); Hugo L. Black, "The Bill of Rights," New York University Law Review 35 (1960):865–881.

25. J. Skelly Wright, "Politics and the Constitution: Is Money Speech?" *Yale Law Journal* 85 (1976):1001–1021.

26. See, for example, American Communications Association v. Douds, 339 U.S. 382, 422 (1950) (Jackson, J., concurring in part and dissenting in part).

27. See generally Rae Langton, "Speech Acts and Unspeakable Acts," *Philosophy and Public Affairs* 22 (1993):293–330.

28. See, for example, Buckley v. Valeo, 424 U.S. 1, 257 (1976) (White, J., concurring in part and dissenting in part); First National Bank of Boston v. Bellotti, 435 U.S. 765, 802 (1978) (White, J., dissenting); Citizens Against Rent Control v. Berkeley, 454 U.S. 290, 303 (1981) (White, J., dissenting).

29. See Black, "Bill of Rights."

30. See Alexander Meiklejohn, "The First Amendment Is an Absolute," *Supreme Court Review* (1961):245–266, p. 255.

31. 424 U.S. 1 (1976).

32. Id. at 48–49 and n. 55.

33. See, for example, Pacific Gas & Electric Co. v. Public Utils. Commission, 475 U.S. 1, 14–15 (1986).

34. 505 U.S. 377 (1992).

35. Id. at 392.

36. Miller v. California, 413 U.S. 15, 24–25 (1973).

37. 505 U.S. at 383.

38. American Booksellers Association, Inc. v. Hudnut, 771 F. 2d. 323 (1985).

39. Alexander Meiklejohn, *Political Freedom: The Constitution Powers of the People* (New York: Harper, 1960; repr. Westport, Conn.: Greenwood Press, 1979), pp. 24–28.

40. Robert C. Post, "Meiklejohn's Mistake: Individual Autonomy and the Reform of Public Discourse," in *Constitutional Domains: Democracy, Community, Management* (Cambridge: Harvard University Press, 1995), p. 268. For a more extended analysis of Post's position, see Morris Lipson, "Autonomy and Democracy," *Yale Law Journal* 104 (1995):2249–2275.

2. ART AND THE ACTIVIST STATE

1. For an important and early treatment of these issues, see Seth F. Kreimer, "Allocational Sanctions: The Problem of Negative Rights in a Positive State," *University of Pennsylvania Law Review* 132 (1984):1293–1397.

2. 135 Cong. Rec. S8807-08 (daily ed. July 26, 1989) (statement of Sen. Helms). For an early discussion of the political dimensions of Mapplethorpe's work, see Ingrid Sischy, "White and Black," *New Yorker*, Nov. 13, 1989, p. 124 (review of shows of Minor White and Robert Mapplethorpe); see also Joseph Wesley Zeigler, *Arts in Crisis: The National Endowment for the Arts versus America* (Chicago: A Cappella Books, 1994).

3. Janet Kardon, *Robert Mapplethorpe: The Perfect Moment* (Philadelphia: Institute of Contemporary Art, University of Pennsylvania, 1988).

4. *Act of Oct. 23, 1989*, Pub. L. No. 101-121, tit. II, S304(a), 103 Stat. 701, 741.

5. 413 U.S. 15, 24–25 (1973).

6. See Jayne Merkel, "Art on Trial," *Art in America* (Dec. 1990), vol. 78, no. 12, p. 41; Isabel Wilkerson, "Cincinnati Jury Acquits Museum Director in Mapplethorpe Obscenity Case," *New York Times*, Oct. 6, 1990, A1, col. 1.

7. See Barbara Gamarekian "Grants Rule Testimony by Arts Chief," *New York Times*, May 2, 1990, C13, col. 1. These pledge requirements became the focal point of a number of lawsuits. One such suit was resolved in January 1991 when the federal district court in Los Angeles held the pledge requirement unconstitutionally vague. Bella Lewitzky Dance Found. v. Frohnmayer, 754 F. Supp. 774 (C.D. Cal. 1991). A second suit, brought by the New School for Social Research in New York, was settled the next month, when the NEA agreed to abandon the pledge requirement for all fiscal year 1990 recipients. William H. Honan, "Arts Agency Voids Pledge on Obscenity," *New York Times*, Feb. 21, 1991, C14, col. 6.

8. *Arts, Humanities, and Museum Amendments of 1990*, Pub. L. No. 101-512, 104 Stat. 1915 (1990).

9. Id. § 103(b), 104 Stat. at 1963. A federal district court in California struck down the law in Finley v. National Endowment for the Arts,

795 F. Supp. 1457 (C.D. Cal. 1992), and an appeal has been pending for three years. The appeal was first argued in August 1995.

10. Harry Kalven, Jr., *A Worthy Tradition: Freedom of Speech in America*, ed. Jamie Kalven (New York: Harper & Row, 1988), p. 401.

11. See Independent Commission, *Report to Congress on the National Endowment for the Arts* (Washington, D.C.: The Independent Commission, 1990).

12. Owen M. Fiss, "A Theory of Fair Employment Laws," *University of Chicago Law Review* 38 (1971):235–314; "Groups and the Equal Protection Clause," *Philosophy and Public Affairs* 5 (1976):107–177; "Racial Discrimination," Leonard Levy, ed., *Encyclopedia of the American Constitution* (1986): 1500–1507.

13. University of California Regents v. Bakke, 438 U.S. 265 (1978).

14. 500 U.S. 173 (1991).

15. Id. at 192–203.

16. Arnett v. Kennedy, 416 U.S. 134, 154 (1974). For a penetrating analysis of an analogous theme in Rehnquist's jurisprudence, see Brooks R. Fudenberg, "Unconstitutional Conditions and Greater Powers: A Separability Approach," *University of California Los Angeles Law Review* 43 (1995):371–520.

17. 500 U.S. 173, 194 (1991).

18. Compare Owen M. Fiss, "State Activism and State Censorship," in *Liberalism Divided* (Boulder: Westview, 1996).

3. THE DEMOCRATIC MISSION OF THE PRESS

1. 376 U.S. 254 (1964).

2. Anthony Lewis, *Make No Law: The Sullivan Case and the First Amendment* (New York: Random House, 1991).

3. See Owen M. Fiss, "Capitalism and Democracy," *Michigan Journal of International Law* 13 (1992):908–920.

4. 376 U.S. at 270.

5. See generally Ben H. Bagdikian, *The Media Monopoly* (Boston: Beacon Press, 1990).

6. For an analogous distinction, see J. M. Balkin, "Populism and Progressivism as Constitutional Categories," *Yale Law Journal* 104 (1995):1935–1990.

7. Associated Press v. United States, 326 U.S. 1, 20 (1944).

8. United States v. Eichman, 496 U.S. 310 (1990).

9. Carnegie Commission on Educational Television, *Public Television, A Program for Action: The Report and Recommendations of the Carnegie Commission on Educational Television* (New York: Harper & Row, 1967).

10. For a general discussion of the background and content of the Fairness Doctrine, see Red Lion Broadcasting Co. v. FCC, 395 U.S. 367, 369–371 (1969). See also R. Randall Rainey, "The Public's Interest in Public Affairs Discourse, Democratic Governance, and Fairness in Broadcasting: A Critical Review of the Public Interest Duties of the Electronic Media," *Georgetown Law Review* 82 (1993):269–372; Thomas G. Krattenmaker and Lucas A. Powe, Jr., *Regulating Broadcast Programming* (Cambridge: MIT Press, 1994).

11. 395 U.S. 367 (1969).

12. Syracuse Peace Council v. WTVH, 2 F.C.C.R. 5043 (1987).

13. Syracuse Peace Council v. FCC, 867 F. 2d 654 (D.C. Cir. 1989).

14. *The Fairness in Broadcasting Act of 1987*, S. 742, 100th Cong., 1st Sess. (1987); H.R. 1934, 100th Cong., 1st Sess. (1987).

15. President Reagan's Veto of the Fairness in Broadcasting Act, 23 Weekly Comp. Pres. Doc. 715 (June 19, 1987). Congress made several more efforts to enact the Fairness Doctrine, but these efforts were thwarted by additional veto threats of Presidents Reagan and Bush.

16. See generally Jerry Berman and Daniel J. Weitzner, "Abundance and User Control: Renewing the Democratic Heart of the First Amendment in the Age of Interactive Media," *Yale Law Journal* 104 (1995):1619–1639, pp. 1621–1629.

17. See Richard A. Posner, *Economic Analysis of Law* (Boston: Little, Brown, 1992); Milton Friedman, *Capitalism and Freedom* (Chicago: University of Chicago Press, 1982). See generally Edward J. McCaffery, "Slouching towards Equality: Gender Discrimination, Market Efficiency, and Social Change," *Yale Law Journal* 103 (1993):595–675.

18. 412 U.S. 94 (1973).

19. This hypothetical is drawn from real life events. Homer Bigart, "War Foes Were Attacked by Construction Workers: City Hall Is Stormed," *New York Times*, May 9, 1970, Al, col. 5; Martin Arnold, "Police Were Told of Plan," *New York Times*, May 9, 1970, Al, col. 6.

20. See generally Burton v. Wilmington Parking Authority, 365 U.S. 715 (1961).

21. 418 U.S. 241 (1974).

22. Id. at 256–257.

23. Columbia Broadcasting System v. FCC, 453 U.S. 367 (1981).

24. 475 U.S. 1 (1986).

25. Id. at 9–17.

26. 2 F.C.C.R. 5043, 5056–5057 (1987). See also Court of Appeals decision, 867 F. 2d. 654, 664–665 (D.C. Cir. 1989).

27. Pruneyard Shopping Center v. Robins, 447 U.S. 74 (1980).

28. Mario Cuomo, "The Unfairness Doctrine," *New York Times*, September 20, 1993, A19, col. 1.

29. 114 S. Ct. 2445 (1994).

30. One section of the Cable Act sought to protect commercial broadcasters, another public ones, but this distinction did not play any significant role in the Court's analysis. Complaining of this lapse, see Donald W. Hawthorne and Monroe E. Price, "Rewiring the First Amendment: Meaning, Content and Public Broadcasting," *Cardozo Arts and Entertainment Law Journal* 12 (1994):499–520; Donald W. Hawthorne and Monroe E. Price, "Saving Public Television: The Remand of Turner Broadcasting and the Future of Cable Regulation," *Hastings Communications and Entertainment Law Journal* 17 (1994):65–96.

31. Turner Broadcasting, at 2471.

32. Id. at 2471.

33. Id. at 2456.

34. Id. at 2457.

35. Id. at 2468.

36. 497 U.S. 547 (1990).

37. University of California Regents v. Bakke, 438 U.S. 265 (1978).

38. Adarand Constructors, Inc. v. Peña, 115 S.Ct. 2097 (1995).

39. 497 U.S. at 617.

4. THE CHALLENGE AHEAD

1. Hurley v. Irish-American Gay, Lesbian and Bisexual Group of Boston, 115 S. Ct. 2338 (1995).

2. Id. at 2340.

3. 319 U.S. 624 (1943).

ACKNOWLEDGMENTS

—

Originally presented under the auspices of Christian Gauss Seminars in Criticism at Princeton University in the spring of 1994, this book benefited from the comments and reflections of many of those who first heard the lectures. In particular I wish to thank Harry G. Frankfurt, Amy Gutmann, Gilbert H. Harmon, Jennifer Hochschild, George Kateb, Andrew Koppleman, and Alexander Nehamas. Victor H. Brombert, the then director of the Gauss Seminars, is due a special debt of gratitude for his warm and gracious hospitality during those days at Princeton. Portions of the book were also presented at Drake University in February 1994, as part of a series sponsored by the James Madison Chair in Constitutional Law. Stanley Ingber was my host there and sometimes critic. I wish to acknowledge his contribution and that of the Drake faculty. I am also grateful to my secretary, Lorraine E. Nagle, and a large number of colleagues and friends here at Yale and beyond who participated in this project and sustained me in countless ways: Bruce Ackerman, Jack M. Balkin, Nancy Brooks, Richard R. Buery, Patricia L. Cheng, Sunny Y. Chu, Gadi Dechter, Zecharias Hailu, Paul W. Kahn, Christopher L. Kutz, Noah B. Novogrodsky, Andrew L. Shapiro, Olivier Sultan, and Nicholas R. Turner. Scholarship is not so lonely, and from this fact comes much of its joy.

INDEX

—